Fiber Expressions
Knotting and Looping

Sarita R. Rainey
Supervisor of Art
West Hartford
Connecticut Public Schools

DAVIS PUBLICATIONS, INC.   Worcester, Massachusetts

Printed in the United States of America
Library of Congress Catalog Card Number: 78-72194
ISBN: 0-87192-107-3

Composition: Jay's Publishers Services
Printing: Halliday Lithograph Corp.
Binding: Halliday Lithograph Corp.
Type: Press Roman Medium and Helvetica
Graphic Design: Bywater Production Services

10 9 8 7 6 5 4 3 2 1

Contents

1 Introduction

Knot tying comes in many varieties and has different meanings to different people. You might interpret knot tying to mean interlocking threads, such as knitting a scarf or dress. Others might feel it is intertwining fibers that make a hard, irregular texture. It could be a group of crocheted loops that interlock or a mass of loops worked in and out of one another. Knotting could also be something as simple as a tied shoelace.

Knotting is all of these things and more. It is a way to create with a linear fiber. It is a way to make a statement in fiber and thread, implementing one's ideas or experimenting.

The origin of knotting and looping goes back a long way. Primitive people used knots for both utilitarian and decorative purposes: to fasten materials to make houses and boats; to trap, harness, and train animals; to make jewelry; to represent letters; to embellish clothing, wall hangings, and tapestries; and to make fringes. The art of knotting takes many forms. It may be different kinds of string construction; it may be cords used to suspend plants, organic shapes, and fiber sculptures; or it may be clothing and personal accessories. Furnishings such as chairs, lamp shades, bottle covers, containers, and screens are other creative possibilities for knotting.

(Left) Knotting and wrapping used as decorative design and accent on Egyptian gown. Collection, Sarita R. Rainey.

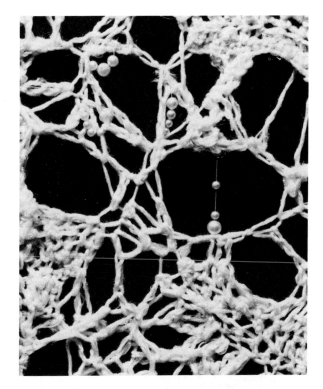

Interlocked crocheted loops. Artist, Sarita R. Rainey.

1

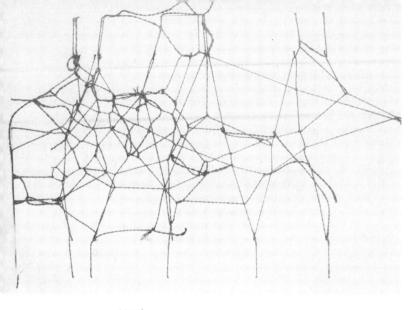

Netting.

Crochet sampler. Artist, Sarita R. Rainey.

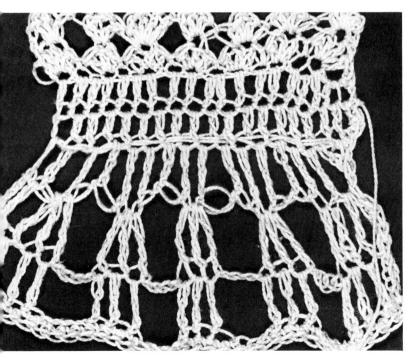

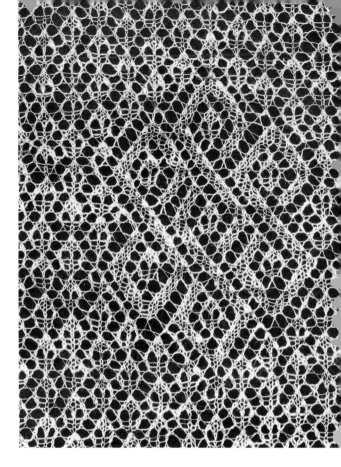

Knitting. Detail of small design from larger piece. Combinations of Alaskan qiviut (musk-ox) and silk, handspun. Design adapted from a 17th-century Peruvian weaving. Artist, Dorothy Reade.

Contemporary loop and knot expressions are numerous. Some more popular forms are netting, crocheting, knitting, and working in macrame. Netting, ancient in nature but prevailing in today's culture, illustrates the simplicity of knotting in its most elemental form. Through the grouping and interlocking of cords, the netting technique emerges into a complex series of open and closed spaces. Crochet, the interlaced loop technique, is enjoying a renewal of interest in fiber as an art form. Crochet is no longer traditional in pattern; it has become experimental in shape and form. Knitting, like crochet, is a loop technique used when creating still other textured constructions with open and closed space relationships. Yet one of the most popular of all knotting techniques is that of macrame — a technique easily understood and used by people of many cultures.

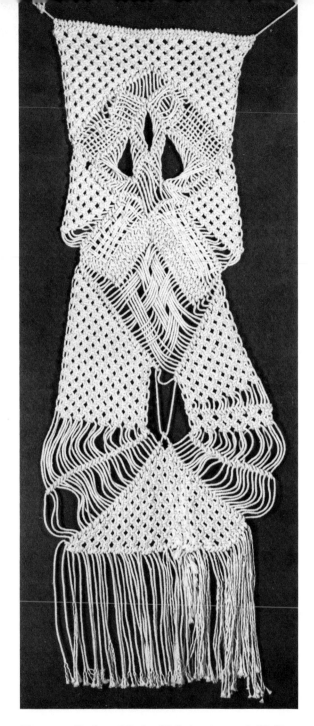

Macrame. Student, Marion Hall Austin, grade 12, New Britain, Connecticut. Teacher, Jane Galt.

The word *macrame* was sometimes used synonymously with the term *square knot*. In fact, macrame is so popular that it is often used as a synonym for general knotting. But knot tying is by no means limited to net making, crocheting, knitting, and macrame. People in numerous occupations work with knots. For example, the knots used by the archer to attach his bowstring, the baker to make pretzels, the butcher to tie meats, the carpenter to sling lumber. Consider the knots used by the jeweler for stringing pearls, the musician for attaching violin strings, as well as those of the surgeon and the rugmaker. Knots are an integral part of life; they touch all of us in one way or another. Further study will reveal that the knot has a long and varied history that parallels the development of civilization.

This book illustrates numerous techniques using knots and loops; it attempts to stimulate one to discover and portray personal expressions. As a source of inspiration, numerous examples of student and professional work are presented to familiarize the reader with techniques and materials. Any single knot or combination of knots may be used to create a pattern. The knotter cannot use all of them at once and should be selective.

Suggestions are provided for creating with knot and loop techniques. Emphasis is on expressions that employ these techniques to communicate with line, rhythm, color, texture, space, shape, and other design elements and principles. No one method, object, or procedure is advocated. Rather, the author suggests ideas and techniques of her own and others' to promote the use of knots and loops as a means of getting started or extending one's visual understanding and creative activity. One is encouraged, through ideas and illustrations, to experiment and discover, to find variations, and to expand one's perception beyond process and technique to aesthetic satisfaction.

Jeweler's knot.   *Musician's knot.*

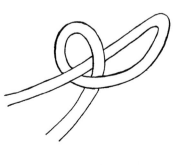

3

2 Design Elements in Action

The elements of design, line texture, color, space, and shape are used in knotting to express one's ideas. Although these elements do not work alone, they are vital to the life and continuity of the total design.

Notice the lines in any knotted or looped construction. Straight lines, curved lines, diagonal lines—each in its own way directs the eye as it moves through the pattern. Single, interwoven, or knotted threads lead the eye through the design. Even a fringe becomes important to the total understanding and feeling of a design. Basically, what exists is a composition made up of the same elements as those in a drawing or painting, differing, however, in the material used and in the application. Unlike drawing and painting and other art areas where line, color, shape, and space may be used, knot and loop constructions exhibit the use of these elements through the manipulation of cords and threads in a tactile way. Basically, a knotted design is a composition of lines, thick or thin, curved or straight, jagged or bent, often enclosing space and creating patterns and rhythms. Knots or loops appear as line when made in rows of repeated crochet or square and half hitch knots. In contrast, knots or loops may appear as rest spots or places to stop the movement of the eye when employed sparsely or at intervals throughout the construction.

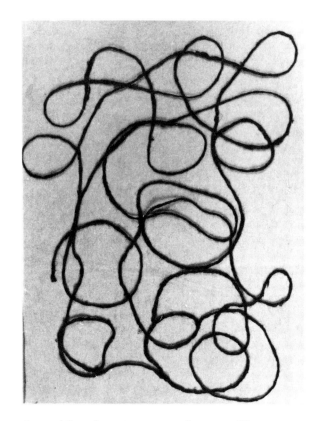

Looped thread creates pattern of space and line.

Student, Janet Anania, Pittsburgh, Pennsylvania.
Teacher, Arlene Sakmar.

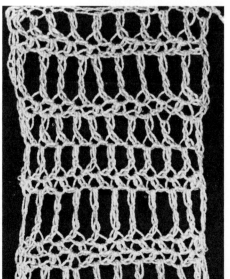

Artist, Sarita R. Rainey.

5

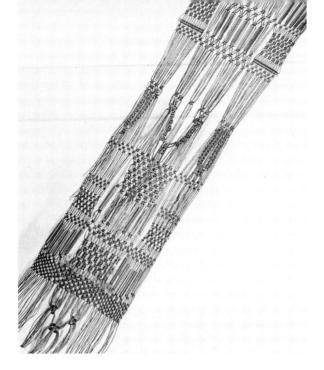

Artist, Hesi Bodlaender.

Line in itself can give direction and simplicity to the pattern. Using vertical or horizontal lines for large areas of the design creates an interesting contrast with more complex parts composed of curved lines and knots of interlocked cords. Also, the simplicity created by vertical lines may be emphasized by using many thin lines of thread that contrast with the feeling of thick lines, such as those made of bamboo.

Texture creates both a tactile and a visual sensation for the designer and the viewer. One must constantly search for all kinds of texture, such as tree bark, seaweed, seashells, feathers, and milkweed, and objects made by people, such as fabric textures of different weaves, cord textures of various sizes, as well as interesting fibers.

The knot artist should have a variety of materials from which to choose a desired texture. One should become sensitive to materials and explore many ways to use them before finalizing a design. When coarse and fine cords, nubby and smooth yarns, threads, leathers, and plastics are employed in different knots and repeated in interesting ways throughout the knotted design, they create a visual as well as a tactile texture. Cords, strings, and yarns of different thicknesses and weights; cords made from natural and synthetic fibers;

and those cords with mixed fiber content such as acrylic and wool give texture to a design. The artist produces raised and incised surfaces, often in combination with flat and plain surfaces, directly through fibers.

Different sizes and kinds of knots create additional textures. Some knots are small in contrast to large, or smooth in contrast to rough knots. Combining knots of different types—the square knot with the curved half hitch, the popcorn with the horizontal half hitch—are other ways to produce both tactile and visual texture. Also, texture can be created when cords are knotted and used in some of the following ways within a pattern:

- alternating rows of square knots;
- even rows of square knots;
- square-knot sennits crisscrossed;
- square-knot sennits woven over and under one another;
- tight-knot sennits in contrast to loose-knot sennits;
- half hitches in vertical, horizontal, diagonal, and curved lines.

Movement in Golds. *Knotted and wrapped sisal with wrapped pieces in gold linen. 5' x 7'. Collection of Winter Park Federal Savings and Loan Association, Altamonte Springs, Florida. Artist, Judith Page. Photograph, Michael Waddell.*

Space exists as a positive thread pattern and a negative area, the area flowing in and around the design. Although space can be sensed and felt by both the designer and the viewer, it must be consciously considered at all times during the creation of any knot pattern. Space between threads and among knots is created when:

- knots of different kinds are combined;
- knots are made in alternating or even rows;
- threads are grouped as solid areas, single sennits, tied, wrapped, woven, or fringed;
- cords and threads of different weights and sizes are used;
- threads are pulled in different directions to create open areas;
- materials unrelated to cords—bamboo or metal cylinders, wood or plastic shapes—are combined to create new spaces.

Shells and feathers accent strands of yarn in different colors and thicknesses. Knotting and floating strands provide a contrast in linear pattern, while the changing directions of the strands create interest. Line is further emphasized with the branch. Artist. Janet J. Farraris.

Accents with Different Materials and Techniques

Materials, techniques, and processes such as enameling, papier-mâché, or stitchery may be combined with knotting to enhance or accent the fiber construction.

A large enameled circular shape as a center focus may appear as a rest spot for the eyes, in contrast to the different line directions of zigzag, horizontal, vertical, and diagonal patterns of the cord. The size of a particular accent, too, is important if it is to be aesthetically incorporated into the pattern. However, when enameling is used, the designer must determine whether to emphasize the knot or the enamel. If the knot is emphasized, the enamel should be small and less significant; if the enamel is emphasized, the knotting should serve as background texture.

Different materials combined with knotting invoke varying emotional responses from both the creator and the viewer. Jute cords and pieces of found metal give the feeling of a rough-and-smooth surface. But feathers often give a fragile, dainty texture when an accent to crocheted yarn and looping, or to weaving and wrapped cords. Other surface enrichments are possible when considering the innumerable materials available. Constructions made with a combination of materials allow the designer to explore a variety of creative avenues. Such constructions may illustrate the use of line, texture, and shape by grouping strands of yarn in varying lengths, by wrapping and looping them in different directions, by wrapping and coiling to produce vertical and horizontal line patterns, and by stuffing shapes to make a single, three-dimensional form or multiple forms within a shape.

Knotting accented with enamel on copper. Artist, Sydel Ackerman.

Artist, Sydel Ackerman.

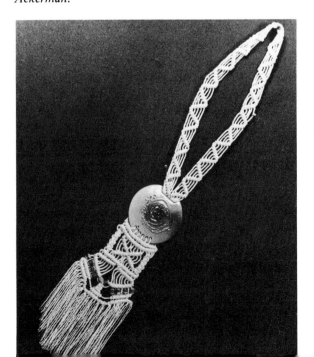

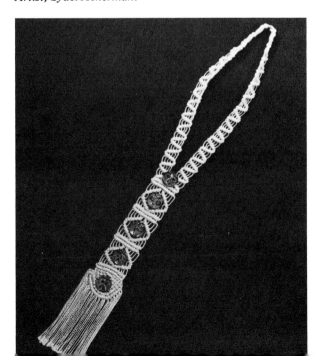

Cotton embroidery floss, beads, and feathers, 3' x 8'.
Artist, Margaret Ballantyne.

Student, Marcie Silverman, grade 12, Kingswood School,
West Hartford, Connecticut.

Construction of suede, cloth, velveteen, creosoted jute,
and olefine wood beads. 2' x 6'. Artist, Judith Page.
Photograph, Michael Waddell.

Dyed burlap, wrapped wool, polyester, stuffed crochet.
Artist, Roslyn Russell.

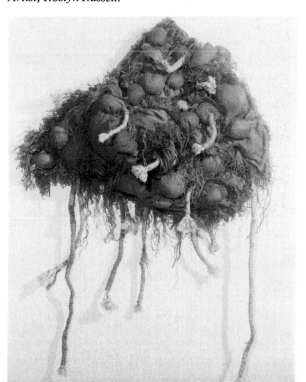

Anatomy of Design

The repetition of one knot interlocked with another, the space relationship between one knot and another knot, and the way one pattern is connected to another are some ways to create the appearance of a complicated and intricate design.

Artist, Sarita R. Rainey.

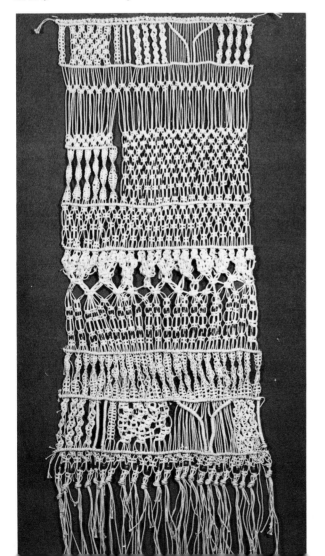

If you have tried to figure out how to make a knot, it soon becomes obvious that following the strands of cord requires concentration. However, you will begin to experiment with different kinds of knots once you learn how easy it is to use them. Combinations of these various knots can then be used to make imaginative, new constructions.

A knot design may be experimental with knotted cords meandering over a pattern; or the design may form centers of interest or textured areas for a stitched appliqué; or it may be a construction of repeated knot sennits and strands of cord. The latter constructions are often symmetrical, with horizontal or vertical repeats. Patterns are often planned to make symmetrical shapes, but they may also be arranged as rows of different lines, different-sized shapes, or variations of texture. Open spaces between free-flowing knotted cords are as important as the knots themselves.

Declamation. *Artist, Gordon MacKenzie.*

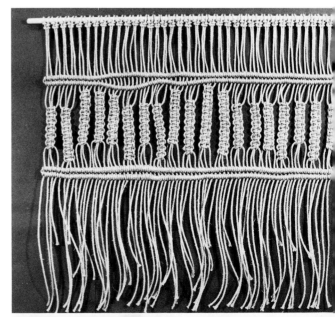

Woven pictures in line. Background and surrounding areas in macrame. Artist, Ann–Mari Kornerup, Denmark. Courtesy, Den Permanente, Denmark.

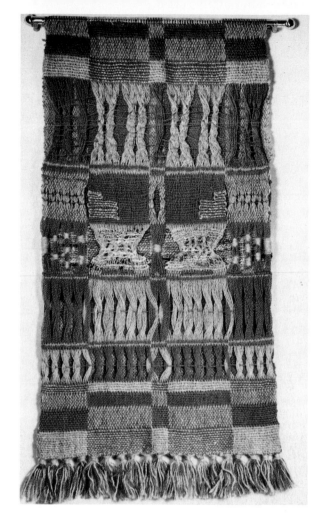

Artist, Betty H. Freedman.

It Is Open Space in Contrast to Line and Shape That Creates Interest. Other areas of interest can be made by combining flat square knots and free-flowing cords with raised half knots in twisted linear patterns or rows of horizontal or diagonal half hitches. Added details such as fringes, beads, feathers, leather, buttons, and clay are useful accents. Still other interest is created by combining different techniques, such as knotting and weaving, or weaving with wrapped threads and knotted fringe.

A knot design may be a series of loops interlocked in various ways to create a form, incorporating a textural surface appearing as unequally spaced lines. Open space in contrast to line and shape is further apparent with simplified patterns that use strands of thread in contrast to sections of multiple frayed fibers. Open

11

space, although negative in nature, may become positive in relation to the total design. Simple lines provide direction and movement for additional interest. By eliminating nonessentials, the artist creates a vital visual pattern.

Design as illustrated and discussed throughout this chapter is only an introduction to the way some designs have been used to portray an idea or emphasize a design element. The simplest of designs may reveal variations in the art elements themselves as a means of interest to the viewer. The outline of an object may be contrasted with the object's surroundings, all of which may be combined so as to form a total shape that will clarify the motif.

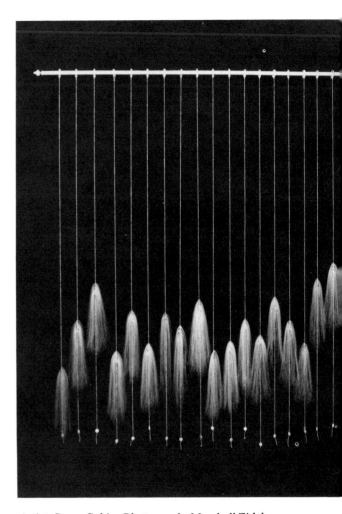

Artist, Norma Minkowitz. Photograph, Kobler/Dyer Studio.

Artist, Susan Sabin. Photograph, Marshall Zidel.

Spear 60'' long. Shield 30'' x 36''. Wrapping. Artist, Gail Kindlund.

Kachina Form. Weaving, wrapping, knotting. Artist, Meredyth Hyatt Moses.

Mask. Wrapped. Artist, Meredyth Hyatt Moses.

Sculptural form, weaving with knotting and wrapping. Artist, Meredyth Hyatt Moses.

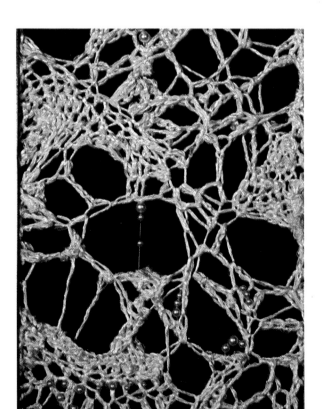

Crochet. Artist, Sarita R. Rainey.

Outdoor environmental weaving and knotting. Student, Westledge School, Connecticut. Teacher, Marge Curtis.

Artist, Gail Kindlund.

Wrapping and knotting. Artist, Joyce Ebert Tidaback.

Wall Hanging. Spokes of wheels used as warp. Weaving, knotting, and wrapping. Artist, Sharon Alexander.

Neckpiece. Knotting. Arlene McCaffrey.

Wrapping and knotting. Artist, Caryl Kaiser Boeder.

Tree, neckpiece or sculpture. Crocheted. Artist, Irene C. Reed.

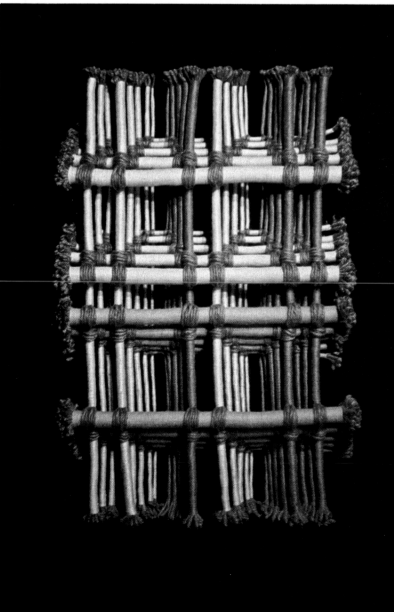

Wrapping and knotting. Artist, Les Bohnenkamp.

Wrapping 50'' x 36''. Artist, Regina Hartzell. Student of Gail Kindlund.

Pendant or brooch. Fabric suffed over cardboard base. Knotted neck piece. Artist, Rachel Love Mitchel.

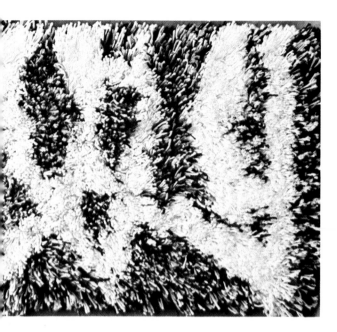

Rug Hooking. Joan Labas.

Wall Hanging with knotted and fringed figure. Artist, student grade 3, West Hartford Public Schools.

Wall Hanging, wrapped. Artist, Jane Knight.

Artist, Barbara Wilk.

Artist, Barbara Wilk.

Sculptural form, wrapped. Artist, Gail Kindlund.

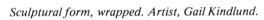

③ Experimental Beginnings

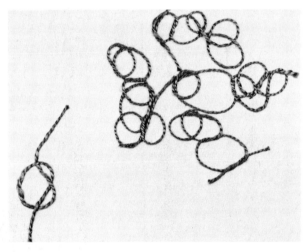

Pasted knots.

Knotted cord used for outlining.

Experimental knots are a good start to more complicated loop constructions. Knots can be used to create interesting textural patterns. They can be glued or pasted to a background, stitched onto a fabric, hung or draped from a rod, or used as an outline.

To make knot patterns, tie single knots, double knots, or triple knots. Combine single knots and triple knots in the same design. Experiment with a different number of knots in the same pattern, alternating the size and the space between them.

Single, double, and triple knots.

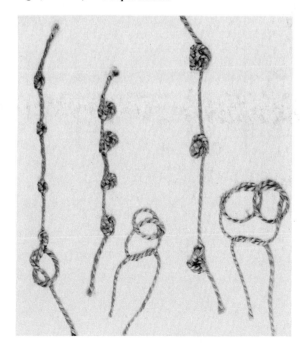

Knots in themselves can be beautiful designs, since line and texture are inherent in their appearance. Yet, for added interest, colored yarn may be looped loosely and pasted to a contrasting background. To vary a knot or loop pattern, change the spacing between and inside the loops. For a nubby texture, pull the loops tightly.

Further variation beyond spacing and texture is possible with inventive use of backgrounds.

- Try cutting or tearing paper to change the edge and shape as illustrated.
- Use knots for accent.
- Try fringing a cloth background.
- Apply knots to a background of reverse appliqué, using the appliqué to enhance the knot pattern.
- Combine stitchery with a knot pattern.
- Experiment with a knot design on a tie-dye or batik.

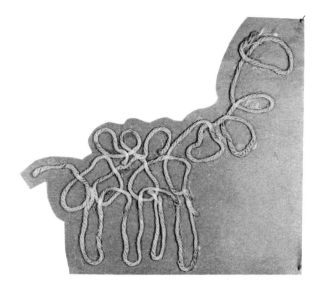

Knotted linear design.

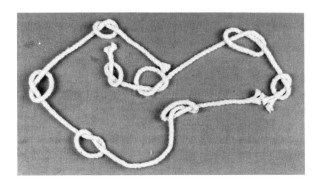

Knotted linear design.

Detail. Knotted cord and silk-screen design. Artist, Sarita R. Rainey.

Knotted linear design.

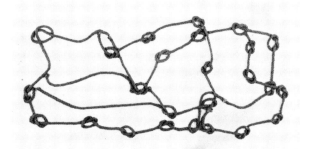

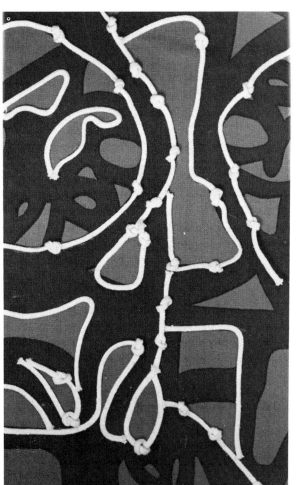

14

4 Wrapped and Coiled Expressions

Down through the centuries, various ethnic groups and cultures have used wrapping and coiling to create baskets. These baskets were used for gathering, carrying, storing, drying, mixing, and serving food. Traditional basketry techniques often employed wrapping bundles of fibers and coiling them together by using one of several types of stitches to join the coils. However, this same versatile technique was used for making other forms, such as furniture, costumes, floor mats, and ceremonial artifacts. The ceremonial body covers worn at Sepik River (New Guinea) village festivals illustrate basketry techniques using bamboo and grass fibers that were interwoven, wrapped, and sealed with clay. Such examples were not only imaginative in design but dramatic in size, ranging from five to ten feet high and fifteen or more feet long.

(Left) Cords wrapped in units. Artist, Jane Knight.
(Right) Wrapping used to connect different fiber units and to give rigidity.

(Left) Wrapping can provide rigidity and body. Artist, Jane Knight.

(Right) Wrapping of cords gives strength to the unit.

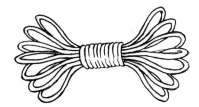

15

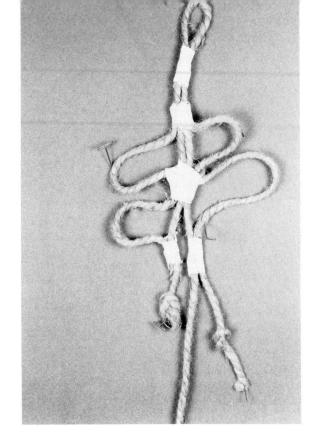

Cord looped and wrapped at points to hold and emphasize the loops.

Simple wrapping may begin by looping a foundation core of binder twine, cord, string, or rope and binding it at selected points. This will emphasize the loops. Playing with cord or string to create different-sized loops will help one discover how easy it is to create both flat shapes and three-dimensional forms. A quick method of binding the loops in place is to cut narrow strips of plaster-imbedded gauze or masking tape and wrap it around the core at specific points. Whereas it is possible to control the shape simply by manipulating with the fingers, additional control is attained by using pins to temporarily secure the loops to corkboard or ceiling tile.

More cords may be attached to the looped cord by wrapping two ends together. Combining different weight, kind, and numbers of cords, such as binder twine with upholstery welting, will add contrast as well as texture.

In addition to wrapping with plaster-imbedded gauze or tape, other wrapping methods may be used. Start by gluing or pasting the end of the wrapping material near the end of the foundation core. A more secure method is to place the wrapping material parallel to the core. Paste the tail end of the material in place, then wrap it over the top of the pasted portion.

Two methods that work well for securing ends of the wrapping material or for decorative purposes are: first, lay the tail of the yarn parallel to the foundation core, wrapping back over part of the tail several times. Make a loop with the remaining part of the tail, and bind by wrapping several times around and under the loop as well as over the tail. Thread the wrapping yarn through the loop, then pull it, as well as the exposed part of the tail, until taut. To obtain a neat appearance, cut off the remaining part of the exposed end.

The second method of securing the wrapping is to bind a group of cords, using one cord to hold the other strands together. When completed, thread the end of wrapping cord through a needle and pull down between the binding and core, snipping off the exposed end.

Wrapping is one of the most prevalent methods of holding groups of fibers together. Specifically, it may be used to bind fibers into one unit, to connect different fiber units, to provide strength within a unit, to give rigidity and body to otherwise flexible units, and to provide contrast in visual and tactile texture. The process of wrapping is easy for anyone to use, yet offers new directions to those looking for a challenge. For these reasons, it becomes an interesting procedure for both the hobbyist and the professional. The wrapping technique also provides a means of extending design possibilities for those with a limited number of materials.

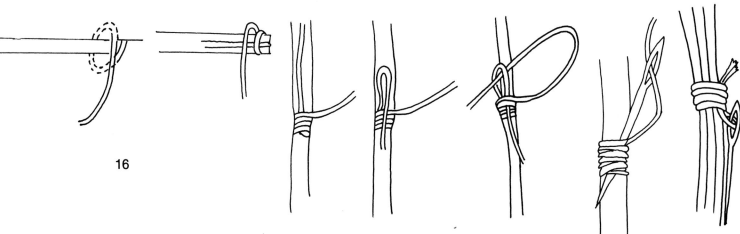

Making Yarn Longer

To add lengths of wrapping yarn, the previous procedure for wrapping may be used. However, in this case, the yarn is doubled to make a loop, then placed along the base cord, leaving the loop ends exposed. Wrap around the middle of the loop several times and pull the wrapping yarn through the loop. Pull the exposed ends of the loop until tight, cutting excess ends to hide where attached.

Still another way to lengthen a strand of yarn is by splicing. Untwist the ends of two pieces of yarn, add a little glue, and twine the ends to be joined by gently twisting them together.

When learning the technique of wrapping, experiment with several types of foundation and wrapping materials, then mount the sample for reference purposes. This may take the form of large cardboard charts that illustrate works by many individuals showing a variety of possible procedures, techniques, color combinations, and textures. Such a procedure is helpful when working with large groups of people, since it makes it possible to quickly visualize a completed work as well as to see the individuality of each person's wrapping.

Wrapping may be as simple as binding strips of wood to make them part of the weaving. Examples of this may be seen in many commercial window shades. Wood strips often are combined to provide color and texture to an otherwise plain blind. Similarly, knotting and wrapped strips of wood may be combined.

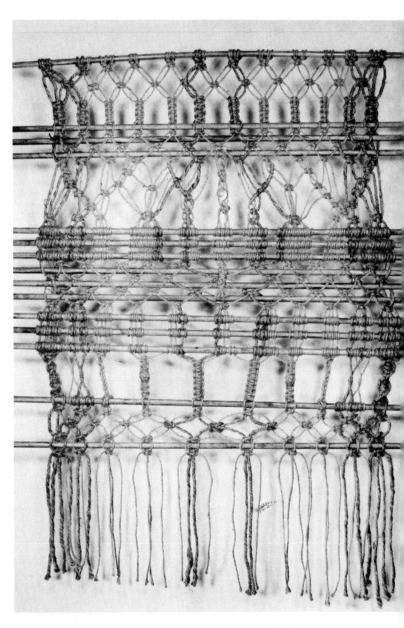

Knotting and wrapped strips of wood. Student, grade 11, West Hartford, Connecticut. Teacher, Bernadine Bailey.

Other ideas are to wrap groups of threads and combine them into a wall hanging or a sculpture, or to wrap cords around a form. Threads may be wrapped in ways that will emphasize grouping and spacing of fibers.

A wrapping technique useful for covering another cord is the half hitch knot. Sculptural forms created with wire armatures may be wrapped by knotting, using the half hitch knot over the wire.

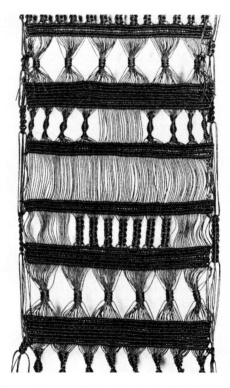

Wrapped threads. Artist, Jane Knight.

Leather with sisal. 60" high. Nylon on wood. 60" high. Wool with sisal. 48" high. Artist, Park Chambers.

Knotting and wrapped threads. Artist, Hesi Bodlaender.

Stoneware sphere shapes combined with knotting, wrapping as hanging sculptural form. Artist, Carol Chesek.

Wrapping

Beyond the many creative possibilities using wrapping, there is the more practical use of holding a base cord to itself when several pieces of cord are combined or when one cord is coiled. Although there are many ways to attach one cord or coil to another, some of the following methods may be useful. These need not be used in any particular sequence.

- Wrap the yarn over and under the bottom cord as indicated in the example, interlocking the stitches of the top cord with those of the bottom. Continue this process for additional rows. To vary the stitch possibilities, interlock into every other stitch or every three stitches.

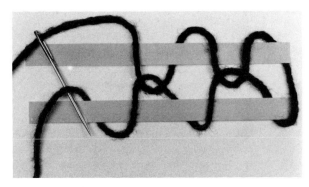

- Wrap yarn over two or more foundation rows at a time. When wrapping is pulled taut, it will hold the different foundation cords together. If variety is desired, wrap the stitches as pairs around two or more foundation cores, leaving space between the pairs of stitches. To double wrap the succeeding foundation core, wrap over one foundation core, then over two cores, alternating back and forth.

- Wrap under and over the top foundation, repeat this on the adjacent row, and continue this process.

- Wrap left to right, under and then over the bottom foundation. Wrap over and under the top foundation, then pierce the bottom foundation and pull the yarn through it. Continue the sequence of this process.

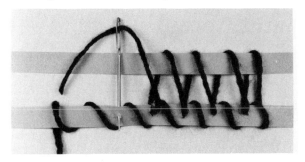

- Loop yarn around the top foundation. Loop yarn around the adjacent foundation, interlocking the loops with those of the above by weaving the yarn over and under them as the loops are made.

● Alternate wrapping under and over the bottom core,
bringing the yarn up over the top core, and behind it.
Then bring the yarn between the rows, crossing over
itself, as a figure eight, then under and over the bottom core. Continue the sequence of the process.

Wrapping, as noted before, is most often employed
with the coiling technique.

Tatting and wrapping. 20' x 6'8''. Artist, Irene Waller.

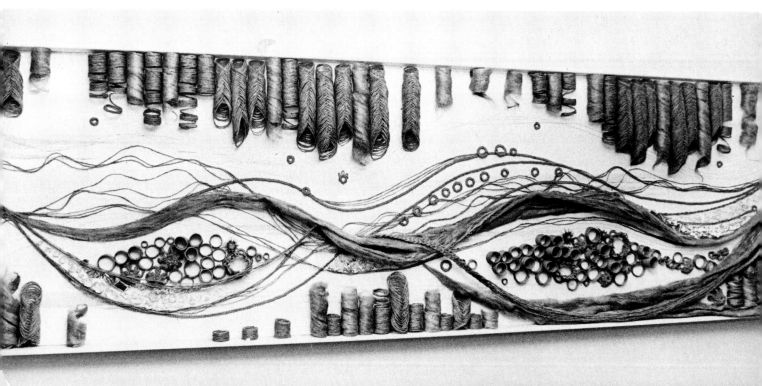

Coiling

Coiling, commonly associated with paper scrolling, claywork, and basketry, is even more prevalent today as a means of creative expression in wall hangings, accessories, and sculpture.

A coiled form may emerge slowly or quickly, depending upon the size of coil used. Thick foundation cores grow more quickly into forms than thin cores. The amount of time will also be influenced by the use of thin and thick coils together; the thicker the coil, the faster the piece evolves.

Using any of the foundation materials (welting, rope, and the like) and the wrapping methods mentioned earlier, begin coiling by tapering the end of the foundation with scissors (see diagrams). Thread the needle with yarn; place the end of the yarn parallel to the taper of foundation material, holding it in place with your fingers; then wrap the yarn back around both the yarn and the core; pull the yarn to tighten. Curve the coil to form a spiral, leaving a tiny opening large enough to insert a needle; or secure the coil by piercing the core and its tip with a needle; hold it in place by a few wraps of yarn. Pull tight, then wrap over it again. Space the wrapping and leave the yarn loose enough to interlock cores and later secure the coils; or cover entire

Detail. Artist, Irene Waller.

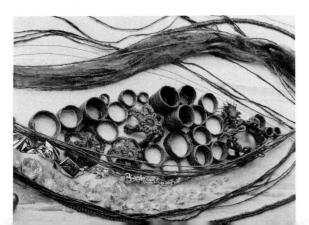

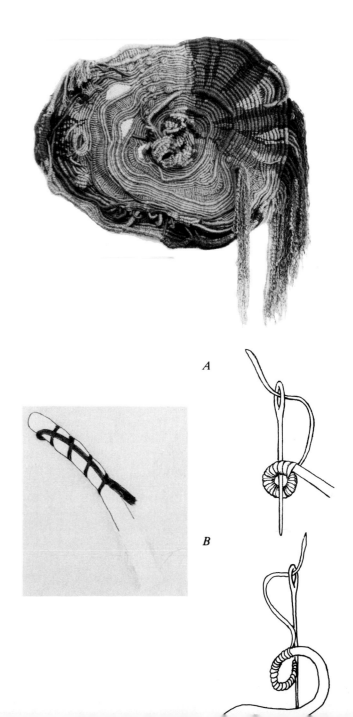

A

B

core with wrapping, leaving the yarn loose enough to interlock the yarn of one core with another, thereby securing the coils. Continue shaping the coil and employing any of the interlocking methods or stitches previously suggested for connecting one coil to another. For example, a common stitch often used is that of the lazy squaw, which spans two or more coils at a time. To apply this method, wrap the yarn around the core approximately four times front to back, then bring wrap from behind and over the core and into the center hole. Continue this process to complete two coils. As the coil gets larger, increase the number of wraps between stitches, inserting the needle over and between the coil next to it instead of through the center hole.

Changing wrapping variations within a piece will result in different stitch arrangements for holding a coil together. Flat forms are made by placing each coil next to the previous coil. Convex forms are made by placing each coil on the outer edge or on top of the previous coil in a position to create the desired curve or slant to the object.

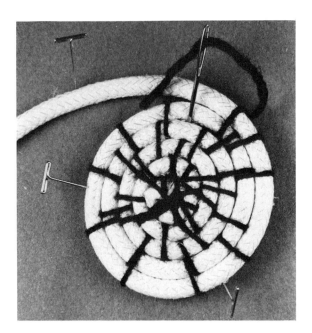 

Small amounts of space may be left between each wrap to allow wrapping from adjacent row; wrapping may be spaced to expose core and provide a contrast between yarn and core; or wrapping may be spaced to create a pattern.

Ovals and Rectangles

Ovals and rectangular shapes are sometimes easier to start than circular ones because there is less spring in constructing the initial coil. Several wrapping methods may be employed. The following ways are only suggestions to get one started.

One method is to lay the tail of yarn parallel with the core, wrapping back over the tail several times as previously suggested in the directions for securing ends. Wrap the yarn around the end and the entire length of the core to secure the yarn. Wrapping may emerge as binding, or as a stitch such as the figure eight stitch. In the illustrated example, the yarn is used to bind the bent end of the core to the rest of the core. Extra security in holding the two rows of core together is provided by inserting the needle into the core and pulling the yarn through.

Another method of wrapping over a core is to first determine the desired length for the center shape. Wrap half of the center length, then bend it in half. The core will be formed at the point where the wrapping stops. Continue wrapping the remaining half. Holding the two cores together, wrap the doubled core as one by inserting the needle under the wrapping of the previous row. When the yarn is pulled taut, the stitch connecting the two cores slips in between the rows.

A third method is to wrap the yarn over about one-half inch of core, beginning about two inches from the end. Bend the core in the center of the wrapped area. Fasten the two cores together by making figure eight stitches back and forth over the entire length of the double core. After each figure eight, pull tightly to obtain a neat appearance and to hold cores securely. At the end of the center core, continue wrapping until the wrapped core can be curved around the end of the center core. Continue figure eights over this and the previously wrapped center core.

Hollow forms may be made spontaneously, allowing shape and size to emerge as one works. However, for forms requiring a predetermined diameter bottom, decide the length and width of the base before starting. To do this, obtain a specific center core length to be used for an oval or rectangular base. Subtract the desired width of the proposed base. For example, a four-inch width subtracted from a six-inch length will have a center core of two inches.

Other Wrapping Materials and Cores

Wrapping material need not be restricted to strands of fiber such as yarn or string. Strips of leather, fabric, pipe cleaners, and wire work well, too. These materials may or may not be wrapped around a base core as previously discussed. They may be attached to themselves, or if they are of a sturdy material such as wire, they can be coiled or shaped to stand alone.

The core used may be expanded to mean any form that provides an armature or support around or on which wrapping may take place. Supports may consist of metal or cardboard containers, clay forms, plastic straws, pipe cleaners, or stuffed shapes.

Sculptural form made with pipe cleaners wrapped around themselves.

Color and Textural Change

Often, when wrapping a base core, one may desire to change yarn color or add lengths of another type of fiber. Such changes offer many interesting variations. To make these changes, place the tail of a piece of yarn parallel to the base core; then wrap back over the core, continuing the wrapping along the core and working the new piece into the pattern. Practice with coiling will lead to other ways of adding yarn, color, and texture.

Other alternative methods for creating color and texture are overlay or embroidery and imbrication.

Overlay

The technique sometimes called overlaying is an interesting way to incorporate contrasting materials, such as raffia, textural yarns, or strips of fabric—velvet, ribbon, or felt—along the core to be wrapped.

Two or three colors of yarn may be used simultaneously and may overlay the wrapping. For example, three different yarn colors might be desired. Lay the tail ends of two different-colored yarns parallel with the foundation core and wrap over them and the core with a third color as in rectangular wrapping. When a color change is desired, pick up one of the two unused yarn colors and begin wrapping over the previous yarn and core. Any number of colors may be employed with this method. Color value can be varied as often as desired to develop interesting wrapping combinations and designs. Likewise, different-textured yarn, string, raffia, or even thin leather may be added.

Color changes create pattern. Artist, Harriett Winograd.

Experiment with different methods:

- Pull the overlay material out between stitches and away from the surface to form a loop.
- Insert the needle between the cores and pull through different yarn colors.
- Embroidery. Apply embroidery (a form of overlay) stitches with yarn or thread over the surface of previously wrapped areas.
- Overlay by stitching previously coiled pieces to a surface.
- Use a blanket stitch to create texture.
  - Wrap yarn around coil.
  - Make loop with yarn.
  - Push needle between cores and up and over loop.
  - Pull yarn tight to secure in place. When tight, the stitch will form a ridge. Adjust with fingers to make a ridge along the side or edge of the core.

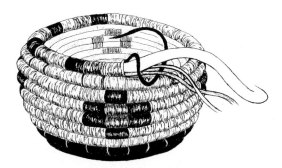

Imbrication

Imbrication, also known as the Klikitat technique, was used by the North American Indians. It is defined as a pattern with overlapping edges, like that of a shingled roof. Imbrication is an interesting way to add color as well as texture. This technique allows one to explore different ways of creating patterns that will offer both a visual and a tactile texture.

Experiment with different methods. As a beginning:

- Lay a selected material along the core to be wrapped as suggested in the section on overlay.
- Wrap the strip or material and the core as a single unit to secure.
- Pull the unwrapped overlay strip out of the way from the core.
- Wrap yarn around core but not overlay.
- Place overlay material back in place.
- Wrap over both flat part of overlay and core.
- Continue this procedure to achieve a pattern. Like the overlay method, the pattern is controlled by the number of wraps and openings between wraps that expose the overlay material. The overlay strip may be left flat or pulled out to form loops on the outside or front surfaces of coiled forms.

Another way to create color and textural change is to expose the foundation core. The exposed core may be used to create contrast in color and texture between the wrap and the core. It also may be used as a means of completing a piece more quickly. To expose the core, wrap yarn around the core, spacing the wraps to expose the area between the wraps.

After exploring the various ways color and textural change might be accomplished, one might consider introducing other materials, not as wrapping, but as attachments or excitement points.

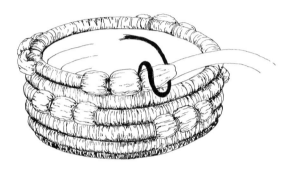

Wrapping accented with looped strips of leather. Artist, Martha W. Gangi.

26

Other Ideas

Artist, Harriett Winograd.

Feathers with wrapped quills. Artist, Martha W. Gangi.
Photograph, Dina Pollock.

Yarn looped and poked between coils, then loops cut to
make fringe. Artist, Martha W. Gangi.

The design possibilities using wrapping can be expanded
by the innovative use of interesting materials.

Pulled threads with yarn looped around sections of
burlap and knotted. Student, grade 4, West Hartford,
Connecticut. Teacher, Johanna McGinnis.

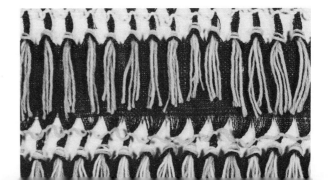

- Add elements between or on surface of the wrapped cores. Feathers with wrapped quill points; leather wrapped flat, looped, laced, poked, or stitched between cores; fringe and various other surface embellishments create a variation to otherwise plain wrapping. The use of different-sized coils along with variations in direction, height, and space relationships, gives contrast, texture, and variation to a plain edging. Feathers and bells provide additional interest, while beads may be the focal point for another. Height is added when wrapped feathers are inserted into a lid and the wrapped cords are looped for handles.
- Add wire. Wrap wire and fiber together to give body. Spray it with lacquer or starch, dip it in thin plaster, or paint it with acrylics.
- Add braiding or fibers. Another kind of interest is created by braiding strands of yarn and adding it as an overlay and hanging attachment from the form itself; or by combining loose strands of fiber with part of the wrapped shape.

Form built of coils looped for handles. Artist, Martha W. Gangi. Photograph, Dina Pollock.

Different-sized coils of different materials provide variation to form. Artist, Martha W. Gangi. Photograph, Dina Pollock.

Coils irregularly looped to make interesting edge.
Student, Donna Achenbach, New Britain, Connecticut.
Teacher, Constance Lebovitz.

Variations created with different-sized coils and wrapped
feather quills. Looped coils at top give height. Artist,
Martha W. Gangi. Photograph, Dina Pollock.

Wrapped welting in sphere form with overhanging
braided fibers. Student, West Hartford, Connecticut.
Teacher, Bernadine Bailey.

Wrapping in double half hitch with loose fibers providing
texture. Artist, Constance Lebovitz.

29

Add parts:

- Combine several wrapped cores to form a wall sculpture or wall pattern.
- Attach looped coils in different directions to create interesting edgings.
- Make several coiled forms. Assemble together to create a sculpture.
- Loop wrapped cores to a prewrapped background or form.
- Attach wrapped cores and coils to different fabric backgrounds.

Artist, Jane Knight.

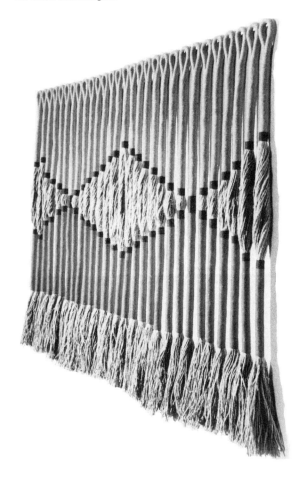

Student, New Britain, Connecticut. Teacher, Constance Lebovitz.

Student, New Britain, Connecticut. Teacher, Constance Lebovitz.

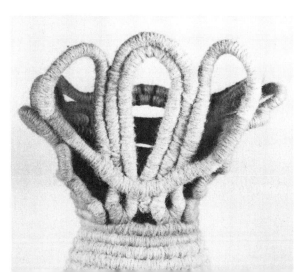

30

Aside from using wrapping as an art form, it also may be used as an accent or to provide variation to an otherwise plain weaving, flat embroidery, or sculptural form. Woven strips of cloth may contrast with the wrapped warp threads. Groups of threads in a weaving are often wrapped to form large cords, thereby forming an essential part of the design as it is incorporated with the final woven piece. Too, wrapped cords may provide three-dimensional effects for a multimedia sculpture of clay, sisal, and string.

Wrapping and coiling are not only useful techniques in themselves but are a fascinating way of using fiber, wire, plastic, or fabric, either singly or combined with other techniques and processes.

Flat sculpture of woven and wrapped threads. Student, grade 5, West Hartford, Connecticut. Teacher, Janet J. Farraris.

Student, Westledge, Connecticut. Teacher, Marge Curtiss.

Bottom part of a container illustrates separate coils attached to top edge. Student, high school, New Britain, Connecticut. Teacher, Constance Lebovitz.

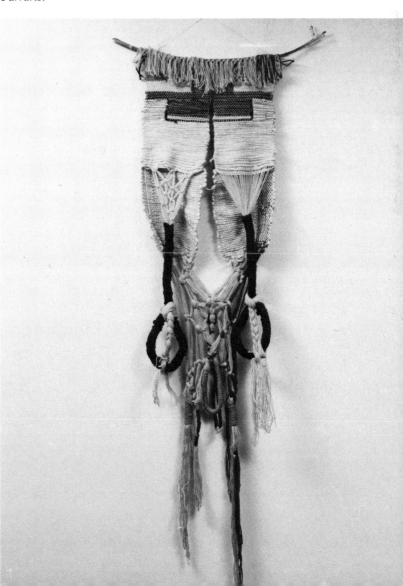

5 Techniques: Netting and Knotless Netting

Netting is an open-mesh construction made by twisting, knotting, or looping at regular intervals. In primitive times, nets served as devices for catching fish, birds, or insects; in Egyptian and medieval times, as decorations on or over garments; in modern times, as environmental decor for windows and walls. Today, in addition to its historical uses, netting is used as barricade devices for games (volleyball and tennis) and as personal accessories for people (carrying bags, hair nets).

For the craftsperson, netting offers knotting and looping possibilities for mesh construction, decorative looping, net overlay, and experimental lacework.

One may begin simple netting by making a series of loops over or around a support, such as cord, rod, or

Fragment: Floral Vase with Deer. *South German, 16th–18th centuries. The Metropolitan Museum of Art. Gift by subscription, 1909.*

wire. Reverse the direction of the loops and thread them under and over to interlock with the first row of loops. Continue the interlocking procedure to join the second row of loops with the third. To vary the loop pattern and provide a tighter interlock, loop under and over a horizontal cord as well as between the loops of the previous row. The pattern may be further changed by looping into the loops of the previous row instead of between the loops.

Another variation of this example is achieved by opening the bottom of each loop of the top row and interlocking adjacent row. Experiment with different loop possibilities. Changing the appearance of a netting pattern is often a matter of adding a twist to the loop or threading a cord through the loops and then knotting the cord to each loop. A tapestry pattern is created when the pattern is worked vertically and the loops interlock where the colors change.

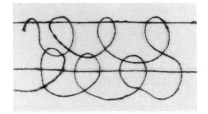

Cover: coarse blue lace darned with white and pointed lace on three sides; geometrical design in squares. Italian, 18th century. The Metropolitan Museum of Art. Gift of Mrs. Magdelena Nuttall, 1908.

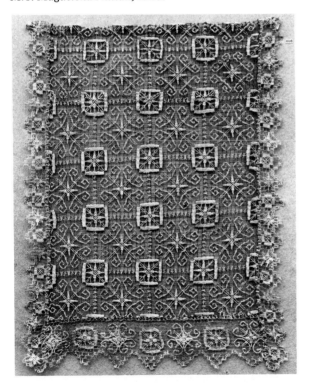

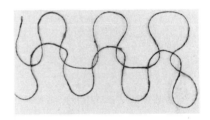

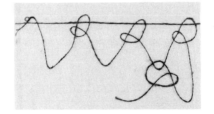

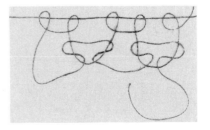

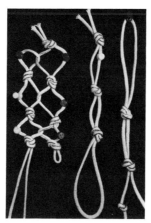

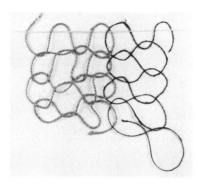

• Make netting over a background fabric, over a string warp or weft.

Devil's Beauties. *Red and rosy cotton and flax yarn lace construction. Artist, Luba Krejci. Courtesy, Museum of Contemporary Crafts.*

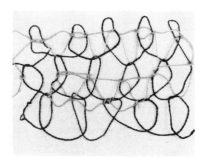

• Net with wire and string over a frame, a branch, holding cord, or the like.

Artist, Matteo Jannicelli.

Netting may be as simple as knotting and interlocking cords. For example, a cord may be knotted with another, then doubled back and threaded between the knots and knotted again as was first done.

Experiment to develop your own innovations.

• Create loose or tight loops.

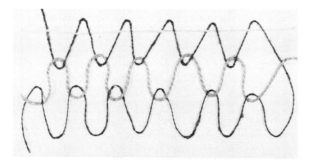

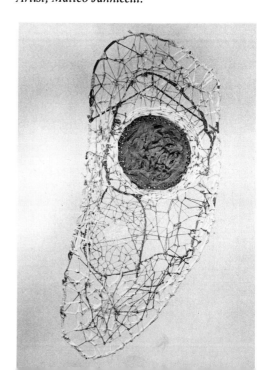

• Crochet strands of chain loops. Combine several loops and stretch over wire to form an armature. Attach threads to armature that later can be looped to create a lacy, knotless netting.

Artist, Matteo Jannicelli.

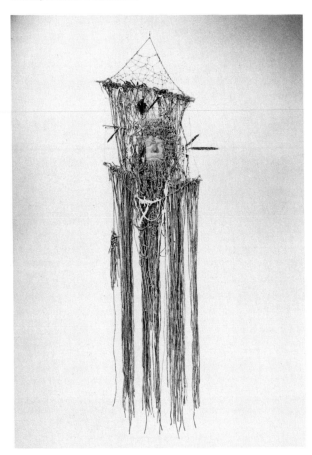

• Attach threads to a frame—an embroidery hoop, a picture frame, or a hand-shaped wire frame.

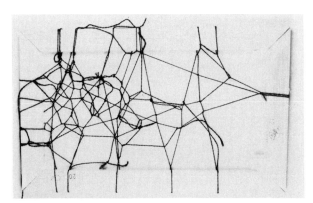

• Use different materials for looping—wire of different gauges or metallic cords.

Artist, Bernard Toale.

• Experiment with patterns of open and closed spaces, tight and loose weaves, thick and thin threads, flat and three-dimensional shapes.

Artist, Virginia Bath.

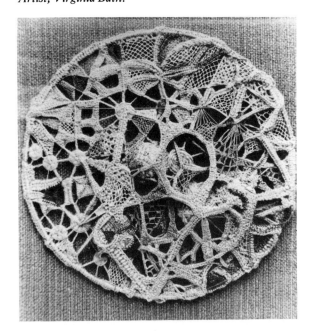

- Combine knotted and interlocked threads with ceramics.

Netting as illustrated with its many loops results in a mesh. Traditional network usually involves the use of such tools as needles and loop gauges (pencil, ruler, cardboard). Plain netting is decorative in itself, but it may be enhanced by adding stitchery, darning, and beads to develop a filet of lace. Innovative netting as suggested in this chapter emphasizes the imaginative use of netting to create mesh compositions in a variety of forms.

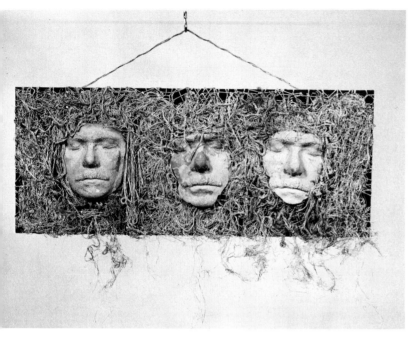

Artist, Matteo Jannicelli.

- Create lace patterns by netting on fabric. Interlock threads at different points to develop interesting space relationships.
- Experiment with two kinds of net pattern: one a single thread composition of space relationships; the other a combination of two or more threads of different weight and color.

Artist, Sarita R. Rainey.

Artist, Sarita R. Rainey.

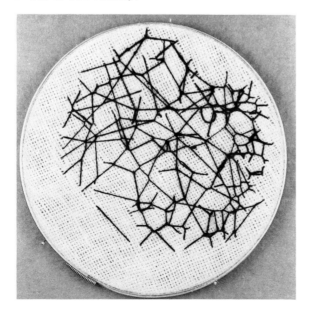

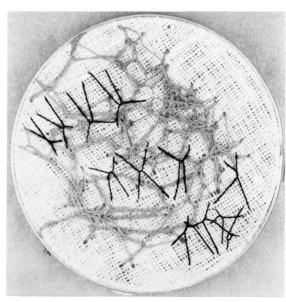

⑥ Techniques: Macrame

One of the most popular forms of knotting is macrame—a grouping of knots in different formations that may vary in size, contour, direction, and dimension. Although old in technique, macrame is a popular way of creating and accenting fiber constructions. People of all ages are experimenting with macrame. People who would never touch a needle and thread, a crochet hook or a paint brush are attracted to this art form. Fingers become the tools, and scraps of yarn or string become the materials.

Equipment and supplies will vary from the necessary items of straight pins, scissors, string, and a branch or stick to the optional items of dowel rod, wire, ceiling tile, T-pins, and mason cord. To begin, one should

select the kind of equipment that best suits one's way of working. Some general information about supplies will provide a start as one searches for items that are appropriate for a particular knot creation.

Pins. Almost any kind of pin will do, especially those with large heads. These vary from pins with glass heads or multicolored plastic tops to T-shaped pins. Another type is the long-shanked corsage pin, which is useful for holding thick cords and heavy yarns.

Holding Bars and Armatures. Equipment used for attaching strings will differ, depending upon the size and shape of the proposed idea. Holding bars (a bar of

Macrame border: Symmetrical floral design with birds. 30'' x 5''. The Metropolitan Museum of Art. Gift of Mrs. Magdalena Nuttal, 1908.

some kind to which cord or string is attached) may vary from a length of cord to a wood or metal rod, or to armatures of varying materials and shapes.

One might begin by attaching string to a horizontal length of holding cord. For straight, simple holding bars on which to mount cords, try a coat hanger, stick, dowel rod, ruler, pencil, or tension rod. The latter is most handy, as it can be quickly placed in a doorway or window and removed when not used. Other suggestions for holding cords are hooks, doorknobs, or hoops.

For some people, much of the creative adventure is creating an armature, such as bending wire into a form or combining pieces of wood to which one may attach and secure cords. Some armature forms may be designed inside other forms, and armature extensions in curves or angles might be added to a basic shape. Tree branches or pre-formed structures of wire, metal, wood, or plastic can also be used to create interesting armatures.

Working Surfaces. Often, manipulation of a cord is easier when it is attached to some type of working surface. Wallboard, Homosite (sometimes called softboard), foam rubber, or cardboard are often used. Wallboard is one of the most convenient surfaces on which to work. Although it can be purchased in assorted sizes and shapes, the most popular is square ceiling or acoustical tile. When used in knotting, it can be held on the lap, carried from place to place, or laid on a table. Pins will easily penetrate the board to hold the cord securely. Wallboard may be purchased with or without a coated surface. To prevent the coating from chipping, pin or staple either cloth or paper over its surface. Also, using cloth or paper that contrasts with the cord will make the knotted pattern more distinguishable and help one better visualize the design as it develops.

With wallboard as the working surface, knotted pieces can be kept taut by pinning the cords and knots as they are made. One need not be limited to a single knot pattern. It is possible to have several tile boards with different macrame patterns in process at the same time. They are easily stored by stacking one on top of another without changing the position of knots or pins.

For large knottings, use wallboard panels, which may be purchased at lumber companies and cut to any desired size. Many discount stores stock precut wallboard in limited sizes.

Although wallboard is the best working surface for me, you may discover other, more suitable surfaces. Examples are a foam rubber slab, a clipboard padded with foam rubber, a cardboard padded with outing flannel, or a cardboard with ends slit to keep the cords in place, similar to that used for a cardboard loom. The top has a slit toward each edge that is used to secure the ends of the holding cord. The bottom has repeated slits for placement of unknotted strands.

Other useful, but not essential, items of equipment are C-clamps to hold the cords in place; rubber bands for the grouping, binding, and shortening of cords; and needles or crochet hooks for pulling and interlocking the fibers. As you gain experience with these supplies, you will soon decide which items best suit your purposes.

Cord. One can make a knot with most any kind of fiber, but some cords will hold a knot better than others. Soft strings and yarns should be used if the piece is to be soft and flimsy. Jute and mason line are appropriate for creating rigid forms.

Some of the various fibers worth considering are fiber cord, clothesline, rope, mason line, seine twine or chalk line, jute, nylon filament, carpet warp, traverse cord, or nylon braid. Trial samples should be explored with different fibers before venturing into any large work.

Prepare the Cord Length. Decide how long and wide you want the finished knotting to be. A minimum of eight cords is necessary for the width or two sennits. Each strand of cord is cut at least eight times the pre-determined length. Add a few inches into your calculations, especially if using heavy yarns or if the piece is to be solid knots. Avoid cutting the cord too short. It's easier to trim any excess after the piece is finished.

What happens if some cords are too short to complete the design? Splice or attach additional cordage to increase the length.

Prepare the Holding Cord; Attach the Strings. To begin knotting, practice by making a sample. Decide how long you want the finished piece to be. Cut three cords: one the desired length for the holding cord, the other two cut eight times as long as the finished piece will be, since these will be used for the knotting. Pin each end of the holding cord to a working surface.

Now you are ready to mount the cords. Double one of the long working cords in half and place the loop over and behind the holding cord, pulling the free ends of the cord through the loop as shown in the diagram.

Repeat this procedure for the second cord. Cords may also be mounted by placing the loop behind and over the mounting cord and pulling the free ends of the cord through the loop. Working cords may be knotted this same way onto rods, sticks, branches, or metal and wood rings.

Choosing One of Three Knots. The three basic knots are the half knot, the square knot (two half knots in reverse), and the half hitch. Repeating any of these knots in a vertical pattern creates a sennit of knots. Some people may refer to these knots by different names. The number of combinations will vary from person to person. Some people combine the half and square knot; others separate them. But for the purpose of getting started, try these three basic knots.

The Half Knot. To prepare the strings for the half knot, four ends are used. Two strings are doubled in half and mounted on a holding cord. The two center cords, B and C, are called fillers. They do nothing. The two outside cords, A and D, are called lead cords and do all the work.

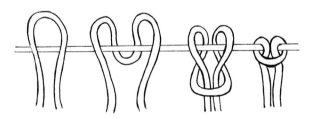

Mounting cord: a. Double cord in half. b. Fold top of double cord behind cord or rod to form loop. c. Place cords at side of fold inside and through loop. d. Pull cords taut.

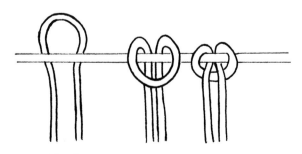

Reverse side of mount.

To begin a half knot, place the right-hand cord D in a backward four (4) *over* the two middle cords B and C, but *under* the far left cord A. Take the A cord, keeping it over the D cord you just brought over, and place it in a four pattern *under* the center filler cords, B and C; then *through* the loop made by the D string. Holding the center cords taut, pick up the two side cords, A and D, and pull the knot tight. Repeating this knot will result in a spiraling of the four-cord sennit.

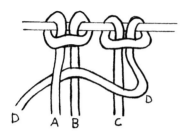

Beginning a half knot.

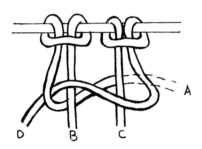

Complete half knot.

An easy way to remember how to make this knot is: *right cord over and under, left cord under and through.*

The Square Knot. The square knot is made of two half knots, the second part of which is reversed. When making the square knot, the procedure is the same as for the half knot. Cord D, in the first half knot, is a backward four (4) D going *over* the two middle cords, B and C, and *under* A. The letter A cord, in a four pattern (4), goes *under* the filler cords B and C, and *through* the loop of the D string. The outer cords are

then pulled tight. Now the change. The second half of the square knot is made in reverse. Cord A is now on the right side and is placed in a backward four (4), going *under* the B–C cords and *over* the right cord. The right cord is then placed *over* the B–C cords and *through* the loop.

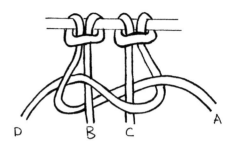

Beginning a square knot by first making a half knot.

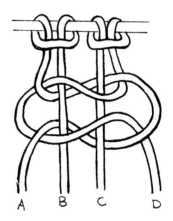

Complete square knot.

In summary, to tie a square knot, the first half knot is *right cord over and under, left cord under and through.* The second half knot is *left cord under and over, right cord over and through.*

Although the square knot is always composed of two half knots tied alternately, either part of the knot may be tied first, depending upon your preference.

If you are interrupted while making this knot, it is easy to forget which half knot comes next. An easy way to remember which half knot you are making is to determine which lead cord is being used (A or D) and alternate that cord's direction. If it is D, as suggested by the illustration, then the D cord would go left for the first knot and right for the second.

Knot Designs Using Square Knots

Different rhythms and widths of line are possible when using only the square knot. The simplicity created with flowing cords connected by knots is easy to see. These examples illustrate how, with imagination, you can vary the positioning of the square knot from an alternate pattern of sennits to a more free-flowing design by utilizing single strands of cord to contrast with knotted sennits.

Knotting may be further varied by contrasting the tension of the cords. Loose knots create space in and between the knots that become an integral part of the design. Tight knots create a solid-appearing positive-negative pattern in contrast to the openness of loose knots. Solid areas of tight knots in contrast to floating cords further illustrate the simplicity of pattern with one knot.

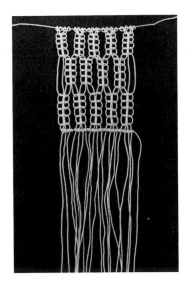

Student, grade 12, West Hartford, Connecticut. Teacher, Bernadine Bailey.

Square knot hanging. Student, grade 8, Montclair, New Jersey. Teacher, John Nace.

Square knot hanging. Student, grade 8, Montclair, New Jersey. Teacher, John Nace.

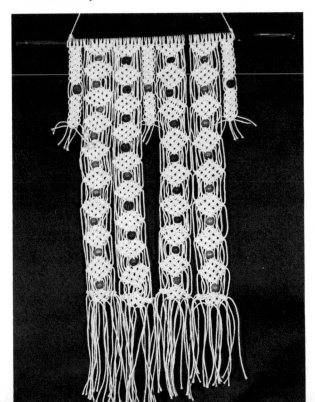

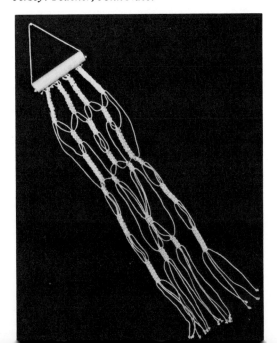

41

Half and Double Half Hitch Knots. The third knot is the half hitch. There are two kinds of half hitch knots: the half hitch and the double half hitch. These are varied by making them vertical, diagonal, or horizontal.

Vertical half-hitch variations.

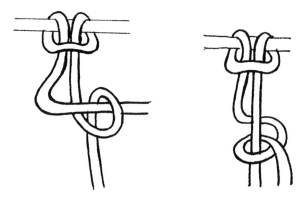

(Left) Horizontal half-hitch knot. (Right) Vertical half-hitch knot.

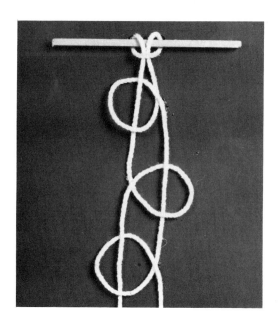

To make a vertical half hitch, first double one cord in half and mount to a holding cord. Using either the left or the right cord, loop one cord around the other to form the hitch. The cord used for looping should be longer. For example, first place the right cord over and under the left cord, then over itself. Then loop the left cord over and under the right cord and then over itself. Continue alternating left and right cords for as many loops and patterns as you desire. See diagram.

Simplicity of knots offer design possibilities of their own. The beginning vertical half hitch may be varied in pattern by doubling or tripling the number of cords, alternating single cords over a double center cord, changing the tension of the cord by tightening the outer strands used for wrapping, or doubling and tripling the loops on each side of the center cord. More intricate half hitch patterns result when loops alternate around a single and double center cord. Other patterns are made by tripling the number of loops or by looping around both the center and side cords.

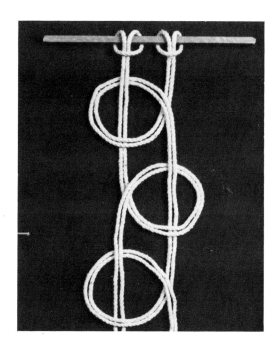

42

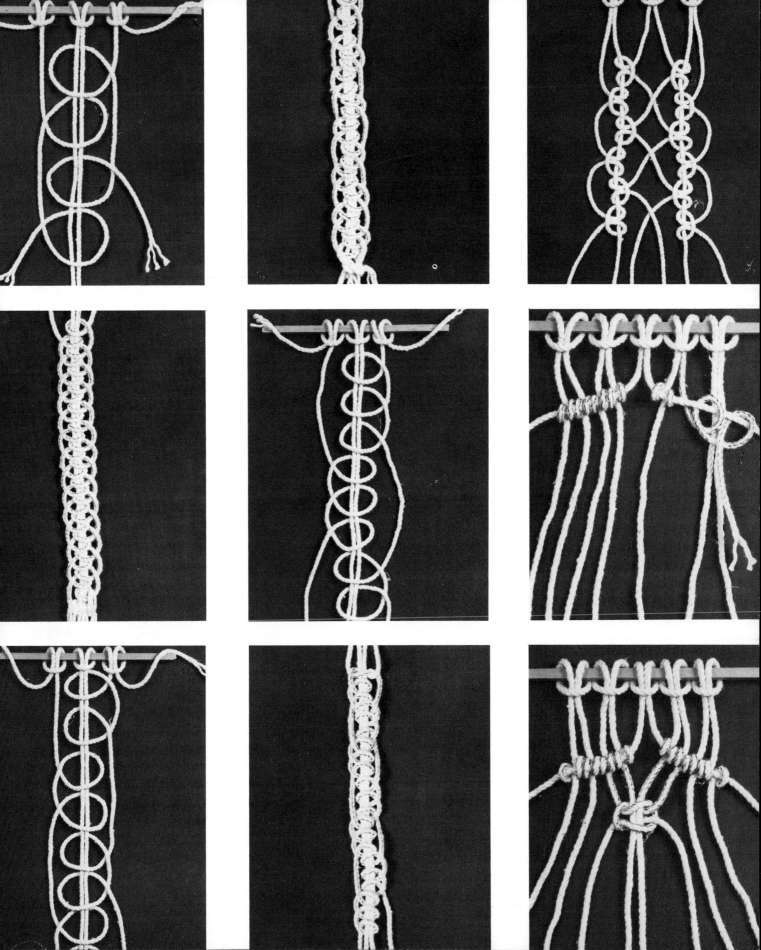

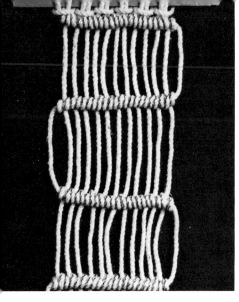
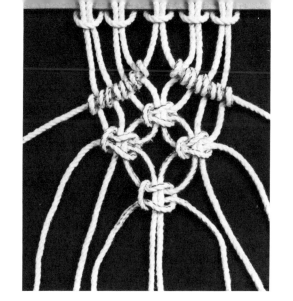
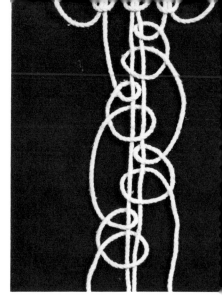

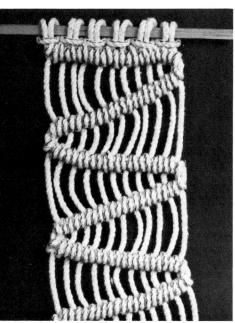

To make a diagonal double half hitch, mount several ends to a holding cord. Make the cords to be used as the diagonal holding cords longer, as these will be the cords to which the other cords are attached. Illustrated here, two holding cords are employed — one to the left and one to the right. The middle left cord shows a completed horizontal half hitch; the middle right cord shows how to begin a half hitch.

Take the end of the right middle cord and make an L shape. Place a pin at the left point of the L and carry the cord over the flat cords. Use the next cord to loop twice over the diagonal holding cord. Continue with the next cord to make the double half hitch, looping consecutive strands until the horizontal strand is covered. Place a pin at the end of the knotting on the horizontal cord to hold it tight. To make a second row of half hitches, reverse the direction, looping each of the dangling strands twice over the horizontal cord. Place a pin at the end of the cord that is hanging full length.

The horizontal half hitch is worked the same as the diagonal and vertical, except it is done in a straight horizontal line.

Experimenting with different diagonal half hitch and horizontal patterns will lead to new design possibilities with line that can be varied or incorporated into flat or three-dimensional designs. Here, the diagonal half hitches emphasize a repetitive diagonal line in contrast to the repetitive unknotted fibers and the textural feeling of the spiraling cluster of half-knot sennits.

Half hitch knots may fill space, provide detailed linear patterns, and create contours. Vertical, horizontal, and diagonal half hitches appear as bold lines in contrast to the multinumber of plain fibers.

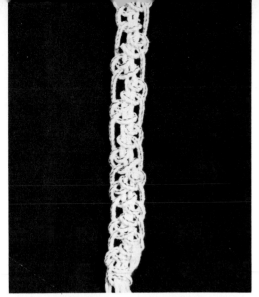

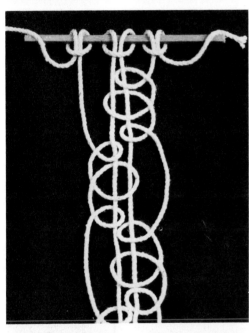

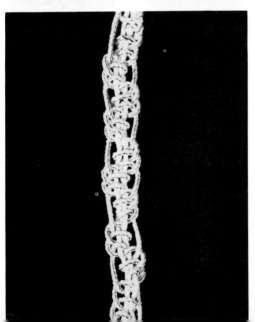

Student, grade 11, West Hartford, Connecticut. Teacher, Bernadine Bailey.

45

Working Approaches

If cords get in the way while working, one does have the option of shortening them. One way to do this is to wind the entire cord around your hand, slip it off, and place a rubber band around its center. Each cord may be individually wound, or if working in only one area, unused cords may be grouped together and bound.

For those who like to work out ideas in advance, preplanning a design is a helpful working approach. However, this method does not allow one to do spontaneous designing as one works.

Creating your own symbols to represent different knots is an easy way to preplan a design. Here a plan is shown whereby the two top horizontals and the related

curve represent half hitch knotting. The U shapes indicate square knotting, and the vertical lines mean free flowing cords. Another example of preplanning is the diagram showing top and bottom half hitches. The

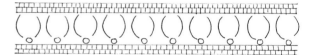

parentheses represent individual knots (square, popcorn, or other ones), and the small circles indicate a single cord overhand knot. When creating one's own symbols, do so with one thought in mind — the easier it is to understand the symbols, the easier it will be to execute the preplanned design.

Student, grade 10, Montclair, New Jersey. Teacher, John Nace.

46

Hangings with Few Knots

Student, grade 8, Montclair, New Jersey. Teacher, Bernadine Bailey.

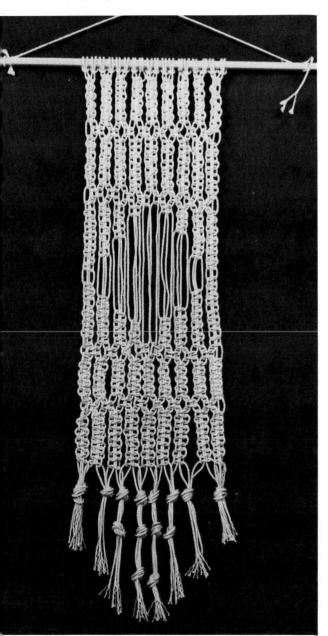

By combining the three basic knots in various ways, a completed hanging can be created. Limiting oneself to one, two, or three knots challenges one's ingenuity. Contrasting vertical lines are created by using plain cords and lines of wider knot sennits. These create a break in the sameness of design and provide textural pattern.

Speculation. *Artist, Gordon MacKenzie.*

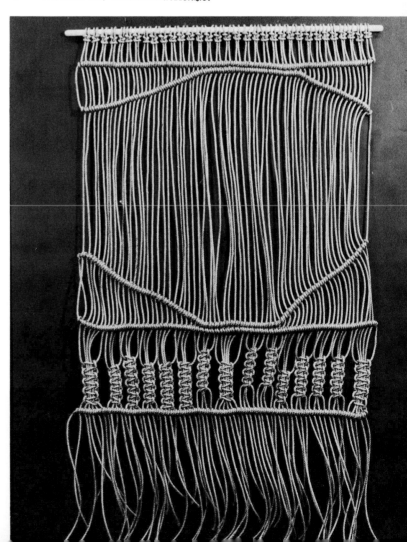

Another approach to the simplicity of linear pattern is the example of horizontal, diagonal half hitch, and square knot sennits dominated by unknotted cords.

More complicated types of knot pattern can be seen in the hanging made with rows of square knots, vertical half hitches, overhand knots, and spiraling sennits of half knots separated by horizontal half hitches.

A designer might concentrate on line by using a half hitch knot to create shape, form, and space. Horizontal and diagonal half hitches emphasize line and shape. Floating cords add a different kind of line, and half-knot sennits provide a twisted line. Square knot sennits crisscrossed and other sennits of different length show additional design possibilities when one or a few knots are employed alone or combined.

Hangings with few knots may dangle as a single unit, may be single units combined into a mobile, or may protrude as a relief sculpture. Since dangling forms are seen from all angles, all sides are important to the design. In the illustrated example, the frayed ends of sisal extend around the form, with all sides being of equal importance. The same is true of the example illustrating horizontal and vertical half hitches.

The idea of using only a few knots need not be limited to wall hangings. The basic three knots may be used to create bottle covers in varied patterns. The design may be started by tying a cord around the neck of a bottle to form a circular holding cord. Square knot sennits are worked off this circle for the first row, then alternated between the previous sennits for the second row. The middle section has a meshwork of alternating rows of square knots. Sennits of square knots are again

Artist, Lucy C. Driver.

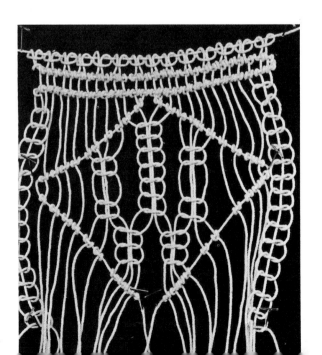

employed to complete the bottle cover. Leaving wide spaces between the sennits allows the bottle to show, creating contrast with the knots and cord. Beads strung on the cord between the rows of sennits provide another texture. The bottle cover is finished by attaching the last sennits to a holding cord that is shaped around the bottom edge of the bottle. In this example, the cord would follow the oval shape of the bottle. Cutting a length of cord and tying it to fit around the bottle, then attaching the sennits to it, will give an ending and finish to the knotted cover. Because the bottom holding cord was made around the bottom edge of the bottle and not under it, the entire cover may be removed at any time and used on another bottle of similar shape.

Other bottle covers may be made as permanent covers. In these cases, the bottom holding cord is placed under the bottom, and all knotting or floating cords are continued and attached to this cord. The procedure might be reversed by beginning at the bottom of a bottle and working upward to the top.

Purses may also be made with just a few knots. They may begin as wall hangings, later folded in various ways, and stitched at the sides to make the purse. The square knot can be used to make the entire form or used as a textural filler. Other purses illustrate a focus on the diagonal, horizontal, and vertical half hitch knots. Variation and uniqueness is added by using multicolored cord, accents of wooden beads, enameled metal, repetitive half hitch patterns or circles, or a large overhand knot with flowing fibers.

Student, grade 5, Montclair, New Jersey. Teacher, Betty Best.

(Right) Artist, Hesi Bodlaender.

Artist, Carol Chesek.

7 Techniques: Rug Knotting

Rug knotting, a useful technique for creating texture and surface enrichment, also involves looping. It offers innumerable textural possibilities, employing loops of different length or loops sculptured by cutting. Although the technique of rug knotting is often considered synonymous with rug making for floor or wall, contemporary artists often combine it with other techniques, such as stitchery, batik, weaving, and the like.

Rug knotting and stitchery combined. Student, grade 5, West Hartford, Connecticut. Teacher, Mary Stenov.

(Left) Artist, Park Chambers.

The process of rug knotting involves the use of a tool with a hooked end to pull and push yarn back and forth through a background material. Also, fingers or a large needle may be used for other types of knots. Textures may be created ranging from shag effects to low-relief sculpture and may take the form of exciting designs for floor or wall accents.

Ideas for design are everywhere: in paintings or prints, cut paper shapes, shapes of buildings, plant life viewed through a microscope, or in many other forms found in nature. The many visual patterns found in our daily lives offer constant and changing sources.

Procedure

Two basic rug knotting procedures may be used as a beginning. The first method involves the use of a backing fabric of burlap or monk's cloth and any one of three tools—the punch needle, the shuttle hooker, or the hand hook. The crochet needle may be used as a substitute for the hand hook. The second method involves the use of a loop-latch hook and a backing material called scrim or rug canvas.

To use the punch needle and burlap in the first method, decide on the rug size; then cut burlap for a backing, allowing several extra inches on each edge for a margin. Use a handmade frame of softwood, a ready-made picture frame, or one of the specially designed stretcher or rug frames. Stretch the backing tightly over the frame and fasten with staples or carpet tacks.

Cut a piece of wrapping paper the size of the proposed rug. With crayon, felt tip pen, or chalk, draw a distinct design that will fill the space inside the margin. Avoid tiny detail that will be difficult to see when working. To transfer the design, sketch directly on the burlap with a felt tip pen or charcoal, paint a design on the burlap with dye, or cut out the shapes and use them as a pattern.

When using the punch needle, thread the yarn through the ring at the top of the handle and then through the inside point. Pull about a foot of yarn through the eye of the needle. Apply tension so the yarn will gradually slip into the tube and handle. Set the loop gauge for the length of loop wanted. Point the open side of the punch needle in the direction the hooking will take. Push the needle through the backing until it hits the handle, keeping the hand firmly on the burlap. Pull the needle back to the surface. Do not jerk, but glide it from one loop to another. Continue the process of punching the needle back and forth through the burlap. When a small amount of hooking has been completed, the loops will begin to hold one another tightly.

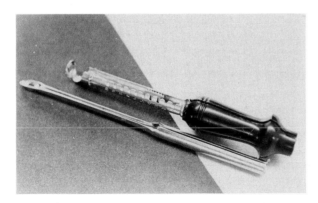

Two parts to needle. They must fit together before threading.

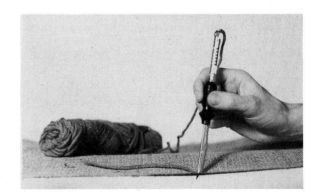

Needle threaded with yarn.

The hooking technique makes a surface that has both visual and tactile appeal. A variety of textures result from snipping the end of each loop, giving the work a velvety appearance; shearing the tops off the loops; sculpturing or shaping the loops, giving a low-relief effect; varying the length of loops, making some high and others low; combining clipped and unclipped loops; or combining yarn, strips of fabric, or leather with the loops.

When all parts of the design are finished, remove the hooking from the frame, then fold back the edges for a neat appearance and stitch to hold in place. Paint latex sizing over the back of the finished piece to secure the yarn to the backing, to give body to the rug, and to prevent the rug from slipping on the floor. If the knotting is to be a wall hanging or enrichment area for another technique, sizing is not necessary.

Completed punch-needle design. Student, grade 6, West Hartford, Connecticut. Teacher, Lucille A. Diorio.

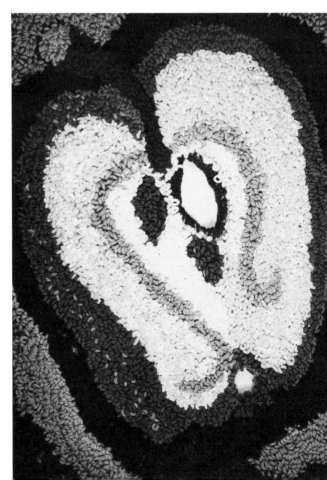

52

Scrim Background

To use the loop-latch hook and scrim in the second method, the latch hook is employed to knot the yarn into the backing. Begin by cutting a piece of scrim, leaving enough material on all four sides to turn back for a finished edge. With a crayon, draw a design on paper to match the size of the rug. Place the paper under the scrim and with a felt tip pen trace the lines of the design on the material. Because of the stiffness of the scrim, it does not need to be placed on a frame.

Cut pieces of yarn the desired length, usually about two inches. To avoid constantly interrupting the hooking process for cutting and measuring, prepare enough pieces at one time to complete a small section. Bring the two ends of yarn together and hold them between the fingers to form a loose loop. Put the hook through the loop and under one strand of the scrim. Pull the two ends of the yarn up to the point of the hook and place them between the hook and the latch. Close the latch and pull the hook back through the scrim and also through the original loop, holding the ends of yarn with fingers to form a knot in the yarn. Continue this process, keeping the loops close together.

This simple introduction to rug knotting suggests the wide range of possibilities this medium offers and forms the basis from which the designer can find his own approach to the work through experimentation. One might begin by exploring other useful knots such as the Ghiordes or Turkish knot. Using a short length of yarn, fold it in half, open the fold and place it over two vertical or warp threads, pulling ends of yarn between and through them to secure the knot.

(Right) Detail of Ghiordes knot made on warp strings of cardboard weaving.

(Far right) Diagram of Ghiordes knot.

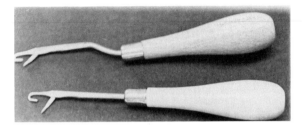

Loop-latch hook.

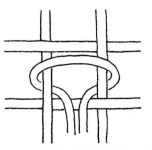

Another knot with possibilities is the Spanish knot. This knot is made by centering a short length of yarn over one vertical or warp thread, crossing the two ends behind the thread, then bringing them to the front on each side of the vertical thread.

An often-used looping technique is that of the Sehna or Persian knot. This knot is made over vertical or warp threads. Loop a strand of yarn around a vertical or warp thread and then pass it in back of and to the front side of the next warp thread.

Stitching knots onto a surface is still another way to create with the rug knot. This type of knot adds interest to flat embroidery or woven textiles as well as useful fringing for points of interest or edgings. By bringing the yarn around vertical threads in a background fabric or the vertical (warp) threads in weaving, a knot sometimes called soumak will give a raised surface and texture.

Variations of soumak techniques may be made by devising different wrapping techniques using a combination of wraps. For example, the Greek soumak knot is made by wrapping each warp or vertical thread three or more times.

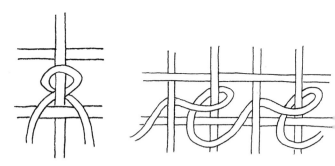

(Left) Diagram of Spanish knot. (Right) Diagram of Sehna knot.

Diagram of soumak knot.

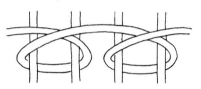

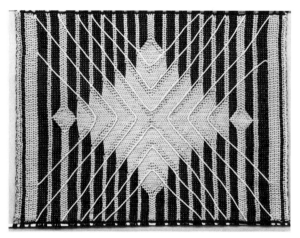

Black–and–white nylon. Soumak technique. Artist, Bodil-Bøtker-Naess. Courtesy, Den Permanente, Denmark.

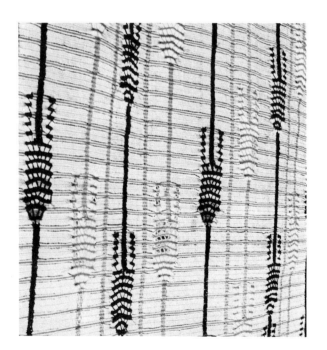

(Left) Soumak knotting on a background of different techniques. Materials of cellophane, thread, cotton, and nylon. Artist, Bodil Bøtker-Naess. Courtesy, Den Permanente, Denmark.

(Left) Diagram of Greek Soumak.

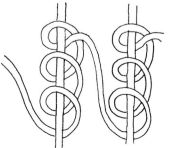

Artist, Donna Braverman.

Discover new avenues, new methods, and different knot combinations. For example, rug knotting provides a textural contrast when combined with other techniques such as fringe effects with weaving. The designer may utilize fingers as tools to knot the yarn onto the warp threads. Yarn also may be knotted onto a burlap background; then the burlap is attached to another background such as felt. Visual statements made by or with rug knotting are many and varied, with patterns ranging from the abstract to the realistic.

Student, grade 4, West Hartford, Connecticut. Teacher Janet J. Farraris.

Artist, Joan Michaels-Paque.

Soumak Technique combined with weaving. Artist, Marge Curtiss.

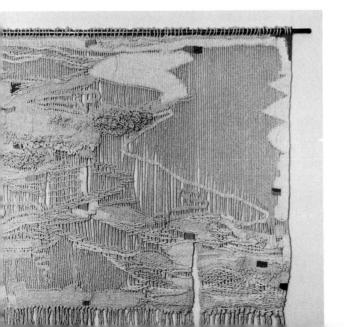

55

Student, Beverly Bryda, high school, Meriden, Connecticut. Teacher, Judith Coutts.

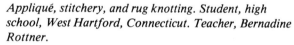

Appliqué, stitchery, and rug knotting. Student, high school, West Hartford, Connecticut. Teacher, Bernadine Rottner.

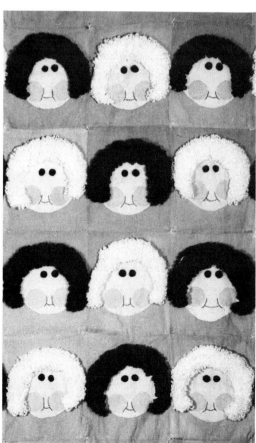

Rainbow Welcome. *Artist, Johanna Jordan. Photograph, Michael Waddell.*

(Left) Wrapping, coiling, rug knotting. Artist, Judith Page.

⑧ Techniques: Chain-Loop Crochet

Crochet, a very old loop-making technique, is a French word meaning to hook or pick. Little is written about crochet's beginnings, and only small lace fragments, suggestive of crochet or the other lace-making techniques of knitting, netting, and the like, have been found.

Crochet, as it evolved through the years, has become intricate in pattern, often appearing as doilies, edgings, dress hems, and wearing apparel. Crochet is currently popular as one of the many fiber techniques for making two- and three-dimensional constructions. The innovative possibilities with thread and hook provide unexplored avenues for the artist/craftperson experimenting with single- and multiple-looped stitches.

The few basic materials consist of a crochet hook, yarn or cord, and scissors. Optional tools and materials consist of the use of fingers to substitute for a hook, a wire with the end bent to make a hook, strands of thread, and wire flexible enough for looping as one crochets.

Branch of tree serves as support over which crocheted chains are stretched. Artist, Beryl Michels.

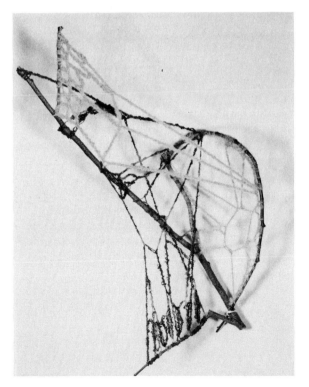

Crocheted medallion of flowers. Swiss, 20th century. The Metropolitan Museum of Art. Gift of Miss Julia Chester Wells, 1910.

Equipment and Supplies

The equipment and supplies needed for creating with crochet are minimal. Most important to the designer is the selection of a crochet hook and the thread, cord, or yarn. Crochet hooks may be made of steel, aluminum, plastic, bone, or wood in an assortment of different sizes. Selection of a hook made of a specific material will depend upon the weight of the cord or yarn.

The following notations offer a guide for choosing a crochet hook to match the thread or yarn: steel hooks for working with thin cotton linen threads and lightweight yarns; aluminum hooks for using regular knitting yarns or heavy cords; plastic hooks for crocheting soft lightweight yarns; giant plastic or casein hooks for using bulky materials; bone hooks (often made of plastic) with lightweight yarns; and wooden hooks for crocheting heavy rug yarns and cords, or, because of their large size, for lace effects with lightweight yarns. The size of each hook is indicated by number. Details regarding these sizes may be found in the next section.

The length of crochet hooks varies from approximately five inches for steel to nine inches for wood. The right length and size of hook depends on what the user finds easiest to use when working with the yarn. Anyone contemplating creative crochet will need to experiment with different hooks and yarns to determine what is best for the item being designed and what is most workable for him or herself.

Emphasis should be on the usefulness of the hook rather than on a specific number or size of hook that may have been suggested by a manufacturer.

Crochet Hooks. The sizes of steel hooks are indicated by number; the larger the number, the finer the hook. Size numbers range from 14, the finest, to 2/0 or 00, the largest.

Sizes are indicated by letter on aluminum hooks, ranging from B the smallest, to K the largest. Size B in an aluminum hook corresponds to size 2 in a steel hook. Size C in aluminum corresponds to size 0 in steel.

Bone hooks are sized by number 1 through 6. Number 1 is the smallest and is equal to size B in alu-minum. Number 6 is the largest and is equal to size F in aluminum.

Wooden hooks also have numbers, but they begin with 10, the smallest, and extend through 16, the largest.

Plastic hooks may be purchased in sizes denoted by the numbers 1 through 10½ or by letters D through K. The letter sizes of plastic may be substituted for those of aluminum and vice versa. However, numbered plastic hooks approximate those of aluminum: 3 equals D, 4 equals E, 5 equals F, 6 equals G, 8 equals H, and so on. Number 7 does not correspond to any letter.

Gauge and Tension. The term *gauge* in crochet means the number of stitches used per inch or the number of rows crocheted per inch. Gauge affects the rigidity of the crocheted form and indicates the density of stitches. The size of the hook in relation to size of yarn determines density. If one uses a large hook with fine-weight yarn, the crocheting will be openlike with less density of stitches. If, on the other hand, one uses a small hook with a large-size yarn, the crocheted form will increase in density. If the stitches appear to be too tight and too many in number, a larger hook size will be helpful. Likewise, if the stitches appear too loose and more stitches are needed for fill-in, a smaller hook size is useful.

Density is also determined by the tension of the yarn or cord as it is crocheted. For example, if one desires a tightly constructed work, the tension may be tightened by adding more stitches per inch. Slackening the tension when working will produce a looser stitch pattern. Tension is a variable that differs from person to person. Some people crochet tightly and others loosely. The important point is that tension is controllable, and it is desirable to determine the amount of tension necessary for the item before beginning. If the item is a free-standing form, the gauge must be dense enough and the tension tight enough to provide body and rigidity to the construction.

Although intricate appearing, crochet may vary in complexity from a series of chainlike loops to triple-loop constructions. A chain consists of a loop through which a thread is pulled to form another loop—the first loop being pulled taut to make a knot. The looping continues with each loop pulled through the previous loop. Since the design is made with a single thread, each loop holding the next loop in place, it is essential that the chain of loops remains intact and unbroken.

Begin your looping by interlooping threads or cords over a supporting structure, using a crochet hook or handmade hook of wire with an end bent to create a hook. If the entire structure is to be covered, follow the preceding diagrams for interlooping. If the support is to be part of the total design, interlock the loops in a repeat process, forming a crocheted chain. A chain of interlocking loops can be any length and can span an open area from one point of the armature to another. Chains can overlap one another and be interlocked into other chains.

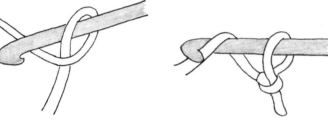

(Left) Make a loop over the hook. (Right) By pulling it taut, a knot will form with a loop left on the hook. Leave the loop loose enough so the working yarn can be pulled through the knotted loops.

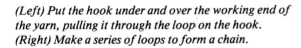

(Left) Put the hook under and over the working end of the yarn, pulling it through the loop on the hook. (Right) Make a series of loops to form a chain.

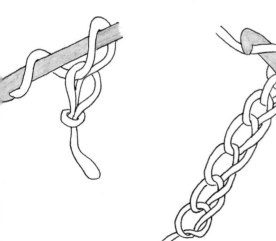

Crochet a chain of loops.

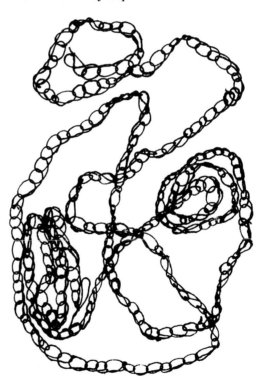

Threads looped over a wire circle using a crochet hook. Fingers may be used in place of a hook when thick cords are employed.

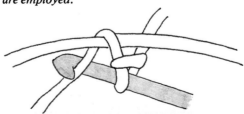

Crocheted chain of loops used to outline a shape.

(Left) Insert the hook into and under the second chain loop from the hook and pull the thread through onto the hook. There are now two loops on the hook.
(Right) Put the thread over and under the hook and pull through both loops on the hook.
(Below) Completed single crochet row. To continue a single crochet, follow the steps illustrated for an entire row of chain stitches. At the end of the row, make one extra chain loop, turn the work to the reverse side, and repeat the procedure for a single crochet.

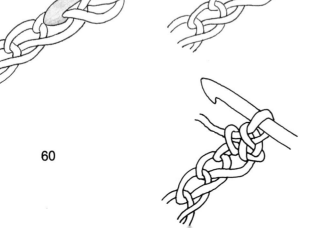

With this beginning, one can develop further techniques by experimenting with crochet, using as few, or as many, loops as are desired for the form you are creating. Or one can combine them in different ways to create the beginning of a crocheted expression. A simple chain of loops may outline or cover an area, as well as form a design of looped lines. Such looped lines can be attached to a background fabric by gluing, hooking through a material (loose mesh such as burlap), or tacking or sewing with needle and thread. Crocheted chains add variety and interest to stitchery when combined with other surface embellishments.

A simple chain of successive loops may later be expanded into many other loops that are changed in size by the tightness and the looseness of the loops. After a chain of loops is formed, a single crochet loop is made by inserting the hook into the second loop from the hook, pulling the thread through it (two loops now on hook), then picking up the thread again and pulling it through the two loops on the hook. This procedure is continued for the entire chain. At the end, an extra loop stitch is made and counted as the first stitch; the work is then turned to repeat the process of the single crochet stitch, eventually creating a solid shape.

Variations

Most crochet stitches are variations of the basic single crochet loop. A versatile stitch for the simplest chainwork or more complicated crochet is the slip stitch. This stitch is often employed as a means of connecting two or more chains or as a way of providing body to an edging. To do this stitch, make a row of chain stitches, insert the hook into the second loop from the hook, then pull the thread through that loop and the loop on the hook. When the row is complete, add one chain stitch before beginning the next row.

Variations can be made by inserting the hook, with yarn over it, through the fourth loop from the hook. When the thread is put over the hook again and drawn through this loop, there are three loops on the hook in contrast to two for the single crochet. Pick up the thread and draw it through two of the loops. This again leaves two loops on the hook. Pick up a thread once again and draw it through these two loops, leaving only one loop on the hook. This will result in a double crochet stitch.

Another variation is to insert the hook through the third loop from the hook. As in the previous double stitch, when the thread is drawn through the third loop stitch, there are three loops on the hook. However, unlike the double crochet, this stitch is made by putting the thread over the hook and pulling it through all three loops simultaneously. To begin another row, make two chain-loop stitches and continue the process.

In addition to different stitch variations, pattern is changed by single crocheting into three chain loops, skipping a loop, then continuing the sequence. Similarly, another effect may be created by crocheting into four chain loops, then skipping two loops.

There are many variations of technique, but what is most important is the ability to use them as one searches for meaningful forms.

Design made with crocheted chains. Artist, Dink Johnson.

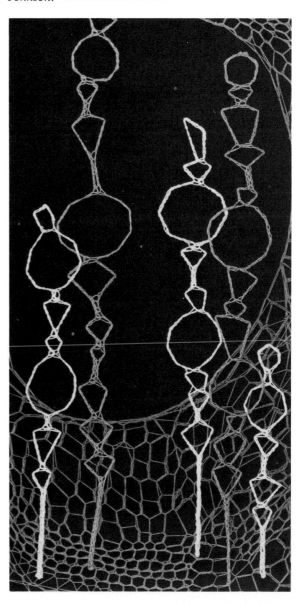

Making Crocheted Fabrications

Armatures. Since a crocheted fabric is soft and pliable, armatures of various materials — wood, Styrofoam, plastic, metal, and leather — are used to give structure. To attach yarn to an armature, knot the cord, leaving a loop, place it over the armature, and pull the end through the knot loop. Pull the yarn taut. Crochet a chain, lapping yarn over the armature for each loop. The entire armature may be covered. A chain of loops may be stretched to span the open space, attaching to another point of the armature. Other support is provided by the way separate pieces are joined, by the way parts are attached to supporting rods, or by stuffing the crocheted forms. Shredded foam rubber, cotton batting, old hosiery, and rags are useful stuffings. Lightweight stuffing is best for crocheted pieces hung on walls or suspended from ceilings.

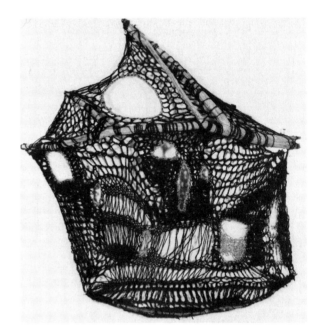

Armature made of a treebranch is exposed under sparsely crocheted yarn. The completed shape is crocheted around another branch at the bottom to weight the yarn and hold the form straight. Artist, Dink Johnson.

Flat pieces joined to create a three-dimensional form, then stuffed. Student, grade 11, West Hartford, Connecticut. Teacher, Bernadine Bailey.

Relief Crochet. Pieces of relief crochet are created by stretching the crochet loops on a frame, over cardboard, wood, softboard, or different armature supports such as branches. Texture is added by rolling the crochet edges, varying the kinds of yarn and stitches, and employing single- and multiple-crocheted chains in looping and dangling strands.

Crocheted tubes of large and small loops joined together and stuffed. Student, grade 5. West Hartford, Connecticut. Teacher, Janet J. Farraris.

Many crocheted creations are made by joining separate pieces or constructions, using a few or several forms combined to create a single unit. Joining is done by crocheting, sewing, or weaving the edges of one piece to another or by stitching one piece to the surface of another. The decision of whether to join two pieces along the edge or by their surfaces rests with the design one desires to achieve. Some pieces require joining the surfaces in order to create a construction of the desired shape and to give it rigidity. If joining a three-dimensional form to a flat surface is wanted, one can crochet stitches directly into the base fabric, connecting the form along its edges. When joining is done along the edges, the following ideas may serve as guidelines:

● Place two edges parallel to one another.
● Insert hook with slip knot through loop stitches opposite each other. Draw yarn through both stitches on each side of edging and through the loop on the hook.
● Continue this procedure to join both edgings as one.

(Right) Joining two- or three-dimensional pieces using a crochet hook to make a slip stitch. Diagram, Courtesy, Dink Johnson.

Separate forms fitted together. Artist, Jane Knight.

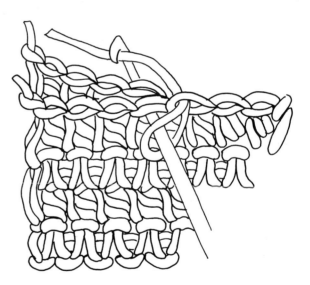

Joining two- or three-dimensional pieces using a needle to make a whip stitch. Diagram, Courtesy, Dink Johnson.

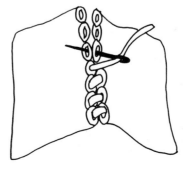

63

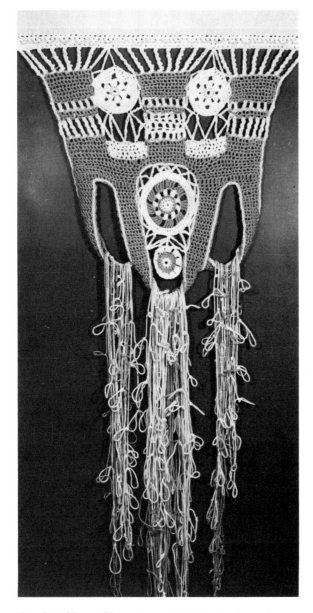

Relief shapes made by increasing and decreasing the stitches. Artist, Dink Johnson.

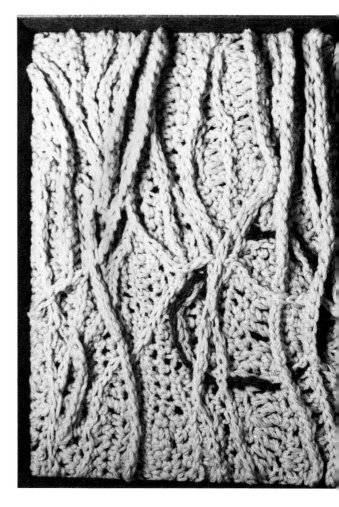

Crocheted looped hanging emphasizing chains and random looping for the fringe. The bottom of a hanging created by grouping yarn strands, then lapping back to front through open areas of hanging, giving a waterfall effect of straight lines that are interspersed with large loops. Artist, Dink Johnson.

(Right) Artist, Sarita R. Rainey.

64

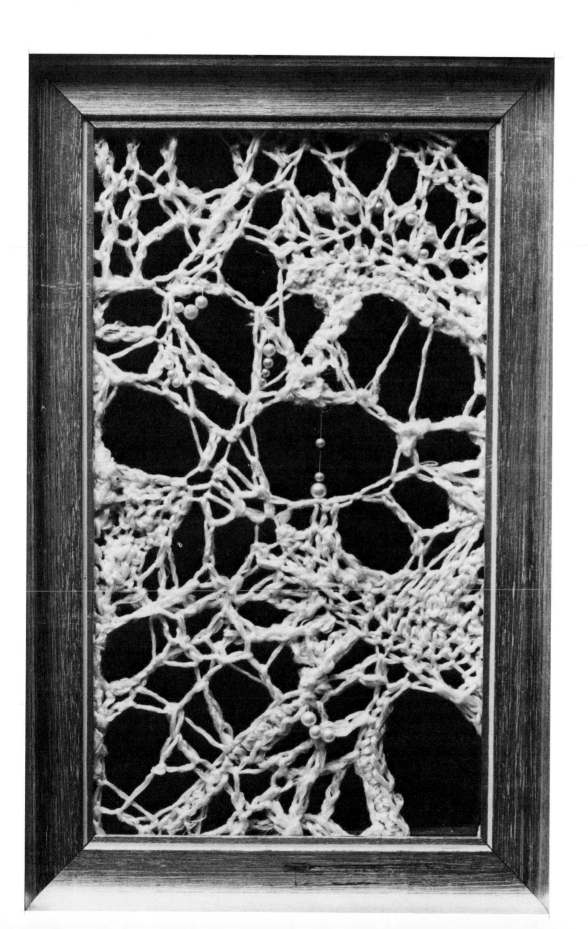

Sculptural Fabrications

Puppet or bottle top cover. Three-dimensional forms joined. Pointed hat is joined to bottom. Puffs on front and top attached with stitching. Collection, Nancy Campbell, Columbus, Ohio.

Three-dimensional forms can be joined to other three-dimensional forms in a manner similar to that of joining relief crochet. Use the crochet chain stitch at such specific points as edges, sides, or top to hold the parts together as a single unit.

Sculptural constructions can be stretched or pulled over plastic, wood, or wire hoops or over a prepared framework or armature; or the constructions may be stuffed. Weights inserted at the bottom of the form create tension to hold the construction taut. Hung as a sculptured group, crocheted forms create an interesting space relationship. There is an interplay between the crocheted shapes and the surrounding space between and among the constructions. The same type of construction may be varied in different ways by employing open areas that are outlined with rolled crocheted edges, braided cords that are crisscrossed and fringed, and stuffed crocheted attachments that also have dangling attachments.

Crocheted fabrications can be ruffled, rolled, and even curved to make intricate appearing forms.

Crochet also may be a suspended hanging, as seen in the example of the sphere, with an interplay of space and shadow created by dangling crocheted forms; or it may be standing sculpture, providing dimension with positive-negative space.

As one becomes adept with crochet loops, some additional techniques may be useful. Shapes in the form of circles, ovals, squares, or tubes increase the potential for both two- and three-dimensional loop expressions.

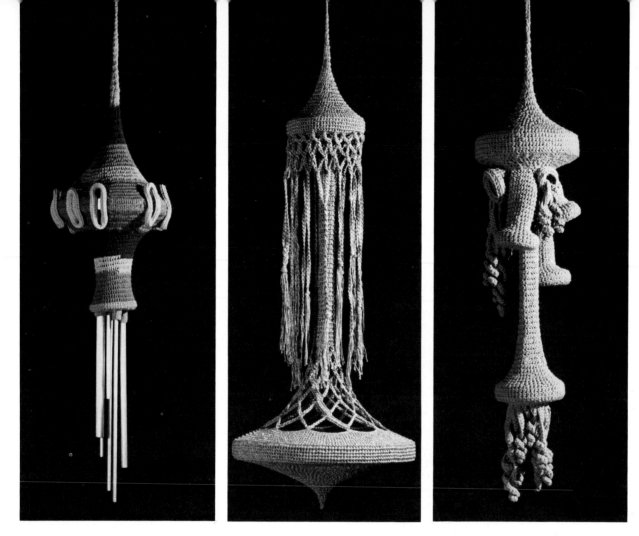

(Left, middle and right) Artist, Jane Knight.

Artist, Bruce Zwingelstein.

Varying a Shape. The shape itself may be changed or varied in size by adding stitches to enlarge (two stitches into one); or by deleting stitches to make it smaller (three stitches on hook, yarn pulled through all three loops). Two easy methods for enlarging are:

- Make basic chain foundation.
- Crochet more than one stitch into each of the basic chain loops.
- Or add one or more extra stitches at end of row.
- Crochet into these and into chain loops of the next row.

Increasing also may be done at any point of the row using the number of stitches one desires.

Deleting stitches, to decrease the size, or changing the shape in other ways, can be done by combining stitches:

- Make a basic chain.
- Crochet into each of two stitches, then combine the two stitches as a final step. For example, crochet into one stitch, drawing the loop through; crochet into next stitch, drawing the thread through (three loops now on hook). Pull the working yarn through all three loops on the hook to combine the stitches.

Still another way to delete stitches is to stop one chain stitch short of the end of the row. The shape will then decrease in size.

(Right) Student, grade 6, West Hartford, Connecticut. Teacher, Joyce Bialczak.

(Left) Crocheted and stuffed spheres connected by chain-stitched loops. Bottom shape stuffed and weighted with stones. Student, grade 12, West Hartford, Connecticut. Teacher, Bernadine Bailey.

Circle Shapes. Circle shapes are made in what is called rounds. As each round is completed, more stitches are added, thereby making the circle larger by increasing the stitches. Many different methods may be used to make circle shapes. A round shape may begin as follows:

● Crochet three stitches into a chain.
● Into the third loop from hook, make seven single crochet stitches.

For the second round:

● Single crochet twice into each of the seven single-crochet stitches of the previous round.

For the third round:

● Single crochet twice into each of the fourteen stitches of the second round.

The number of increases from this point must be determined as one works. Increases in size may be achieved by alternating rows of single crochet with rows of single crochet increases. Increases may be made at every second stitch, every third, or every fourth stitch.

Circle shapes may begin in still another way. Crochet a number of chain stitches; then form a ring of stitches by connecting the two end stitches with a slip stitch. From this point on, one can crochet into each of these chain stitches, using single, double, or even triple stitches. Join the end with a slip stitch.

Sisal and feather, employing weaving and crochet. Artist, Roslyn Brown.

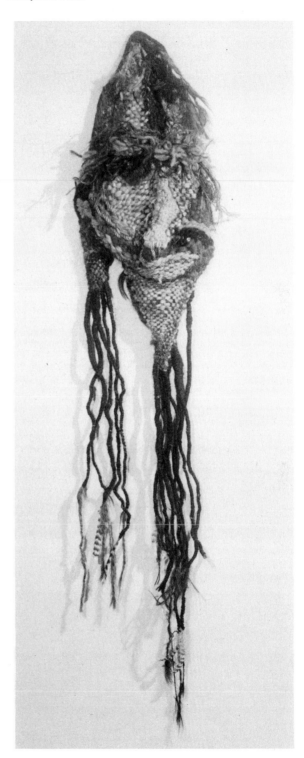

Experimental Ovals. Oval shapes are made by single crocheting a chain the desired length and adding stitches at the ends of the rows. If the oval begins to curl, add more stitches to the ends to increase the size of the shape. Experiment making a spiral oval:

- Determine the length of the inside of the oval shape.
- Make the desired number of chain stitches to match length.
- Add one chain stitch for turning.
- Insert the hook through the second chain and single crochet.
- Continue single crochet into each chain loop back long the chain.
- Increase by making four single crochets into end stitch, then work back along the other side of the chain to the end.
- Repeat the same number of end stitches used on the first side.
- Continue to increase size of oval by adding chain stitches to ends and crocheting into them.

Bowl Shapes. Bowl shapes begin as a circular base made of a series of crocheted rounds joined together. To make the sides of a bowl form, continue crocheting rounds, but make each round smaller. The circle shape will then begin to turn into a bowl shape. To make parts of the form larger, increase stitches to make the shape go outward.

Bowl shapes also may be constructed by crocheting around such objects as a bowl, bottle, or high-sided dish. These serve as armatures for supporting the shape. The crocheting may be left over the armature as a decorative cover. If a free form is desired, remove the piece from the armature and coat the inside of the crochet with a combination of one part white glue and one part water or acrylic polymer. When the mixture of glue and acrylic polymer dries, it will add stiffness to the form, thereby allowing it to stand upright.

Sculptural forms can be made by combining bowl shapes into a single form. The shapes are first stuffed to make them sturdy, then stitched together to make a sculpture.

Tube Shapes. To begin a tube-shaped crochet, make a basic chain and join the ends with a slip knot. Single crochet into each chain loop. Continue this process, working all the way around until a tube shape begins to form. A tube shape can be varied by crocheting increases on one side or crocheting extra rows of stitches.

Three Graces. *Crochet, plastic box, leather, wire. 9" x 6". Artist, Norma Minkowitz.*

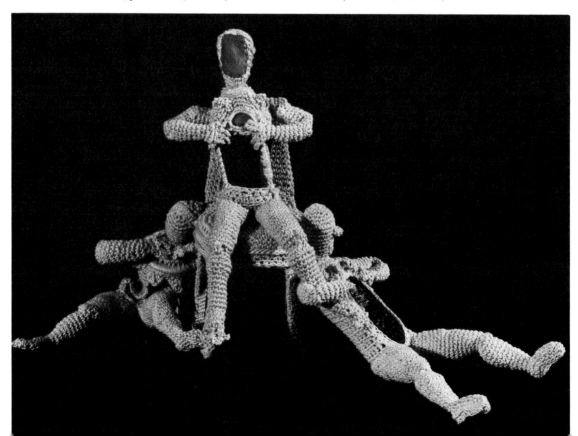

⑨ Techniques: Chain-Loop Knitting

Another kind of loop construction is made by knitting. This technique of combined interlocking loops creates an open or closed pattern and, like crochet, is portable and easily carried from place to place.

Much has been written for the active knitter, using patterns and directions of many kinds. The purpose here, however, is to focus on knitting as an art form with emphasis on loop design and free-form constructions.

Basic materials needed for the knitting loop construction in this chapter are a frame made with wooden strips, nails and a hammer, either cotton or wool yarn, scissors, and dowel rods that can be used as substitutes for knitting needles. Optional materials are knitting needles, yarns, pins, a ruler, and needlepoint guards.

The simplest beginning in knitting may be experimentally pursued using a knitting frame and nails. To make the frame, cut two pieces of wood, approximately two inches wide and any desired length. Space the two pieces about three-fourths of an inch apart,

then nail another piece of wood under both ends to hold the long pieces in place. Place nails about one inch apart along the length of the long pieces. The nails should be approximately one-half inch from the inner edges.

To begin a knitting loop construction, knot the yarn around the first top left nail. Pull the yarn down and around the bottom of the nail; up, over and around the second top nail; and so on. Continue winding the yarn until all of the desired number of nails have been used. Begin to wind the yarn back toward the left end of the slot. As the yarn is wound over the nails, the first strand is pulled up, over, and off the nail to form a loop. Continue this process for each nail. As the knitting progresses, the work is slipped off the nails and through the slot opening. When enough loops have been made to form a fabric of loops, remove the yarn from the nails. Interlock each loop as it is removed with fingers, needle, or crochet hook to prevent unraveling.

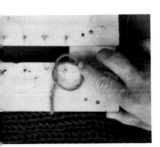  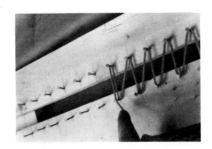 

Knit construction made on wood frame. Artist, Dink Johnson.

Knitted constructions can be varied by looping the yarn several times around the same nail or different nail combinations. To emphasize the open and closed spaces made by looping, stretch the knitting in different directions over a flat surface, a wire form, or a support such as papier-mâché.

More traditional knitting is done with needles, which are generally inexpensive. Needles, straight or T-pins, needlepoint guards (to prevent work from slipping off the needle when idle), scissors, safety pins, and a ruler are all you need to begin. Needles vary in material, length, and thickness. They may be purchased as straight needles, with single or double points, or as circular types. Needles may be made of metal, plastic, wood, bone, or shell. An inexpensive but handy needle, especially when no equipment is available, may be made of a wooden dowel rod sharpened with a knife at one end and sanded. Dowels of small diameter may be pointed in a pencil sharpener. Dowels also are good to use when working with slippery yarns that tend to slip off metal or plastic.

To begin traditional knitting, yarn is cast on one needle (in a varying number of stitches), with a second needle inserted to make successive rows of stitches. See

diagrams. Once you understand some basic stitches, the difference between crossed and uncrossed stitches, and the direction of stitches (left needle stitches determine direction of right needle stitches), knitting may be used to create both flat patterns and three-dimensional forms.

There are many variations of stitches with needle and yarn. Experiment with yarns of different stretch factors, long and short stitches, loose and tight loops, tight and long stitches, and single and double stitches. Try tension sections in contrast to stretch sections. Explore enrichment techniques such as knitting into the same stitch, knitting three stitches in one, or wrapping specific stitch sections.

Reprinted from Coats & Clark Book 190–A Learn to Knit.

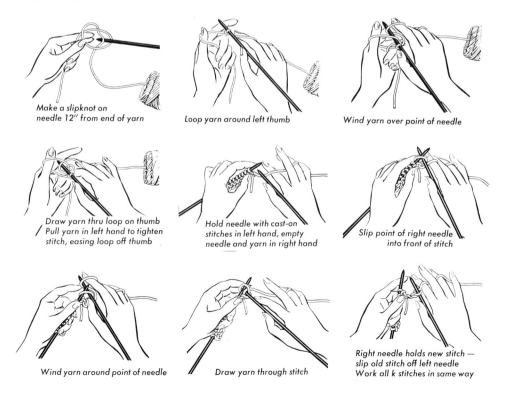

Make a slipknot on needle 12" from end of yarn

Loop yarn around left thumb

Wind yarn over point of needle

Draw yarn thru loop on thumb / Pull yarn in left hand to tighten stitch, easing loop off thumb

Hold needle with cast-on stitches in left hand, empty needle and yarn in right hand

Slip point of right needle into front of stitch

Wind yarn around point of needle

Draw yarn through stitch

Right needle holds new stitch — slip old stitch off left needle Work all k stitches in same way

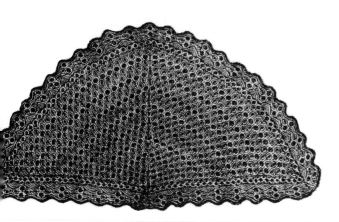

Artist, Dorothy Reade. Photograph, courtesy, A. C. Reade.

Artist, Ferne Cone.

Artist, Dorothy Reade. Photograph, courtesy, A. C. Reade.

Experiment with loops in tight and loose constructions. Combine shapes of different width and stitches such as stockinette (alternating rows of knit and purl stitches) and garter (knitting every row).

Explore different repeat shapes within a shape.

Try making cylindrical shapes. Knit onto round armatures to provide body and structure to form.

Reshape flat knitting by inserting wire at various points and bending into three-dimensional forms or irregular flat shapes.

Stretch flat knits onto a background of softboard and pin in place.

Experiment with different types of armatures—Styrofoam, stuffing (cotton, hosiery, yarns), and the like—to serve as supports for knit constructions.

Try creating different patterns of line and space.

Student, grade 12, West Hartford, Connecticut. Teacher, Barbara Rouleau.

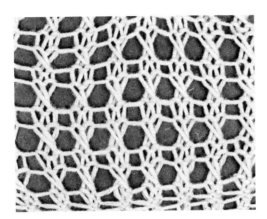

(Above) Cast on even number of stitches. Row 1—Purl. Row 2—Knit second stitch on needle, leaving it on the needle, then knit first stitch. Remove both stitches. Continue across the row (this makes a crossed stitch). Repeat these two rows of pattern. Openness increases with size of needle. Artist, Mary Bailey.

(Below) Row 1—Knit. Row 2—*K 1, yarn over needle twice, repeat from * across row end K 1. Row 3—*K 1, drop the 2 yarn over, repeat from * across row. End K 1. Row 4—Knit. Repeat these four rows as often as needed to obtain desired length. Laciness depends on size of needle. Artist, Mary Bailey.

Knitted form stuffed with foam rubber. Student, grade 5. Teacher, Joyce Bialczak.

74

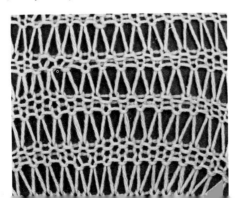

10 **Mounts**

Mounts, like painting frames, are more than an extra attachment to a knot or loop construction. They often are overlooked, ignored, or considered only as an afterthought. However, the mount should be incorporated as part of the construction. Mounts come in many shapes and sizes. They may be simple cords attached to another cord, complex handmade pieces, and found objects.

The simplest mounts, other than cord, are rods. These range from wooden dowels to curved branches. The branch with its gracefulness becomes an integral part of the knot construction.

In one example, the knotted cords and branch appear as a natural part of the environment. Yet in another example, the knot sections are spread over the entire length of branch with parts of knotting separated by spacing the cords at different points on the branch. The stretched cords, due to spacing, expose the branch and shapes within the form.

Mounts, like those used for jewelry, should enhance a construction and be integrated with its knot or loop formations. Some mounts are made by bending reed or wire, or cutting and shaping metal. Others are found objects—hoops, tools, bolts, rods, handles, or animal bones. A hoola-hoop works well as a support for knotting and looping strands of fiber. Creating different and spatial relationships within the hoop, as well as around the edge, provides interest. The hoop itself may be exposed or covered with fiber. Strands may dangle

Student, Marion Austin, grade 12, New Britain, Connecticut. Teacher, Marge Curtiss.

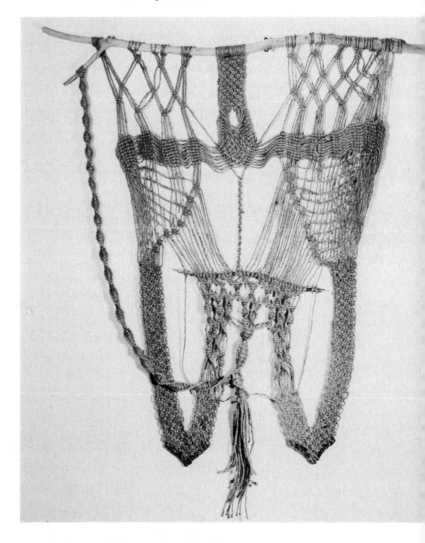

From the Land of Oz. *Weaving and wrapping, 9' x 13'.*
Artist, Yael Bentovion.

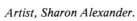
Artist, Sharon Alexander.

(Above) Artist, Lucy Schnider.

(Below) Artist, Candy Miller.

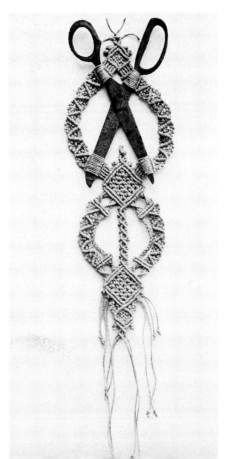

76

Knotting on old railroad tie bolt. Artist, Candy Miller.

from the hoop, or fringe may be added to the circular shape. In each of these pieces the knotting and the mount work together as a total piece. For example, when scissors were used, the knotting was started at the top and the cord wrapped around the scissors as the knotting was continued downward. When an old railroad tie bolt was used, knotting was attached to the bolt and worked downward. When the piece was complete, knotting was added to the top. A final accent was added by wrapping wire with jute to give a corkscrew effect at the top and bottom. Feathers were added when the piece was done.

Still other found items are specific objects searched for to provide unusual combinations between knotting and object—horse bit, singletree, or yoke. These items may focus on a particular relationship among elements, in this case objects relating to a horse. The oxen yoke and horse harness hames—curved pieces of wood lying on top of the collar of a horse harness—illustrate two approaches to using similar mounts. The ox mount utilizes knotting, while the horse hames have yarn attached with knots and fibers wrapped between the hames. In the latter example, the straps, links, and trace tugs that are part of the harness are incorporated into the total design.

A mount may also be a preshaped form over which a knot or looped construction is stretched or set. For example, wheels provide interesting ways to mount fibers. These illustrations show how the wheel, wrapping, and knotting are combined as a total design. The iron buggy spring shows another type of preshaped mount.

(Right) Knotting and wrapping on wheel. Student, grade 11, West Hartford, Connecticut. Teacher, Barbara Rouleau.

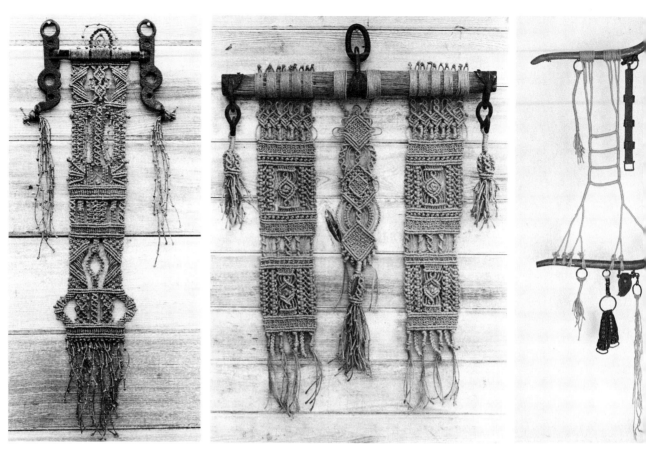

(Left) Knotting on horse bit. Artist, Candy Miller. (Middle) Knotting on singletree for hitching horses. Artist, Candy Miller. (Right) Knotting on horse harness hames. Natural jute and spun afghan\hound hair. 6' x 2½'. Artist, Peter Belmont, Jr.

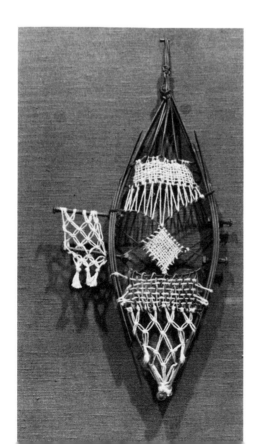

Knotting and looping on iron buggy spring. Artist, Clara Creager.

Handmade Mounts

Handmade mounts vary from a reed or wire bent into a shape, to more complex organic forms. Some possibilities:

- Combine reed shapes such as circles and crossbars to make a skeleton on which to attach threads.
- Shape wire as a circle from which to hang cords, or attach pieces of wire together to integrate with looped threads.

Artist, Gail Kindlund.

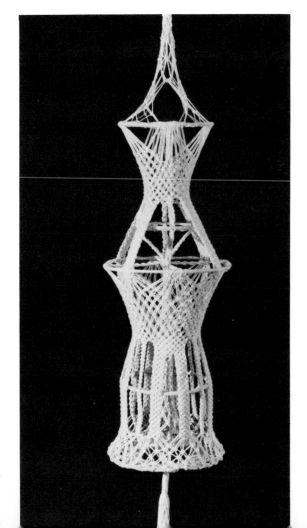

- Make wood frames and stretch threads over and around the edges.

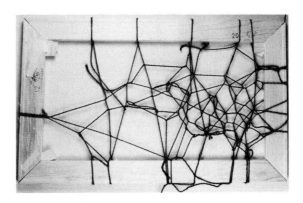

In process. *Artist, Sarita R. Rainey.*

- Cut strips of metal, drill holes along edge for placing cords, and bend into shape.

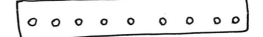

● Pierce areas of flat metal.

● Bend wire into shapes.

● Combine separate wire shapes to form new shapes.

- Create a clay shape with open areas for attaching cords.

- Make bottle-shaped covers of clay and pierce holes along edge to hold cords.

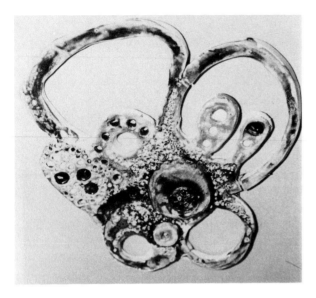

Clay form made for mounting cords. Student, grade 5, Montclair, New Jersey. Teacher, Betti Betts.

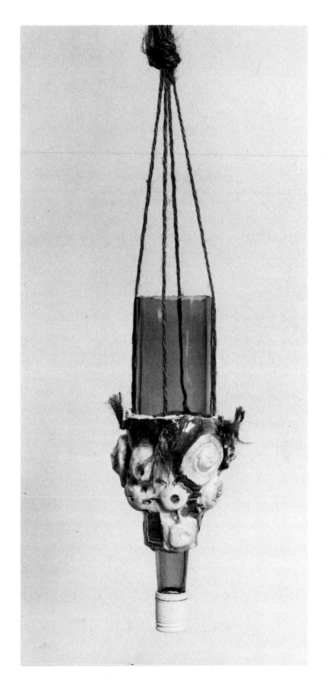

(Right) Student, grade 5, Montclair, New Jersey. Teacher, Betti Betts.

Self-supporting Constructions

A self-supporting construction has the rigidity that will allow it to hang or stand on its own. Wrapping is one way to provide such rigidity.

Coiling is another way to provide rigidity. Separate sections, when combined into one unit, strengthen the total piece. Individual pieces, such as the head with one coil attached to another, easily stand on their own.

Rigidity is also apparent in examples having stiff protruding parts.

Still other fiber constructions, because of their tightly knotted fibers, are rigid enough to make them hang flat against a wall.

Tightly knotted or looped constructions are capable of standing alone.

Artist, Constance Lebovitz.

Artist, Joan Michaels–Paque. Nylon fiber. 8'' x 16''.

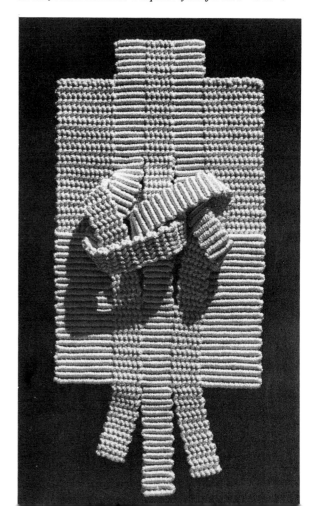

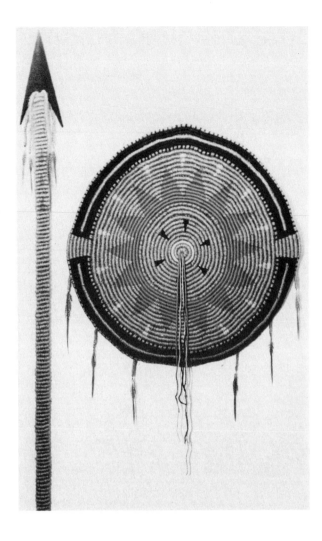

Coiled and wrapped. Artist, Gail Kindlund.

(Right) Bird Seed Bag. *Crochet. 7' x 17'. Artist, Norma Minkowitz.*

Three-Dimensional Dangling Mounts

Many fiber expressions are knotted or looped over three-dimensional frame-type supports to serve as ceiling hangings. Often such supports are preshaped embroidery hoops, or wire shapes of circles, ovals, or squares. Experiment with ideas. As a beginning, try some of the following:

● Group cords together in a single knot; wrap or loop loose cords over different-sized wood or metal embroidery hoops.

Student, grade 5, Montclair, New Jersey. Teacher, Eileen Scally.

● Emphasize strands of thread in contrast to circular hoops.

Artist, Gail Kindlund.

● Attach cords to a circular wire and knot downward to make a cylinder; attach more strands to circular wire and knot upward to make top section of cylinder. Join separate knotted pieces to create side shapes. Add long strands of fiber as accents.

Plant holder. Plexiglass and knotted cord. Artist, Arlene McCaffrey.

● Experiment with bottle hangers, working top to bottom. Bend the wire to match the shape of the planter bottom. Make a loop with cords to begin hanger; add a ring or wire circle to add interest; design dangling mount for holding; separate cords as you work. Begin knotting downward and end design by knotting over prebent wire to match the shape of the planter bottom; add more cords at bottom to provide dangling strands.

Student, grade 6, Montclair, New Jersey. Teacher, Eileen Scally.

● Design container hangings, working bottom to top. Make a circle with cord or wire to fit center bottom of container or bottle. Attach cords to circle and work upward over the bottle.

Other Mounting Possibilities

Marionettes with control bar and strings may also be employed as a kind of hanger. In this way, the marionette, though now used as a wall hanging or suspended construction, is still available for use as a puppet.

Stuffed burlap form on pedestal accented with feathers, weaving, and wrapping. Artist, Roslyn Brown.

Marionette. Student, grade 12, New Britain, Connecticut. Teacher, Constance Lebovitz.

Some mounts are merely base supports. Such supports might be made of sheet or solid plastic, wood, or metal. Tree stumps or natural bark attached to a box offer other possibilities.

Pre-formed containers and sheet metal cut and shaped will provide still other frameworks within which to attach fiber constructions.

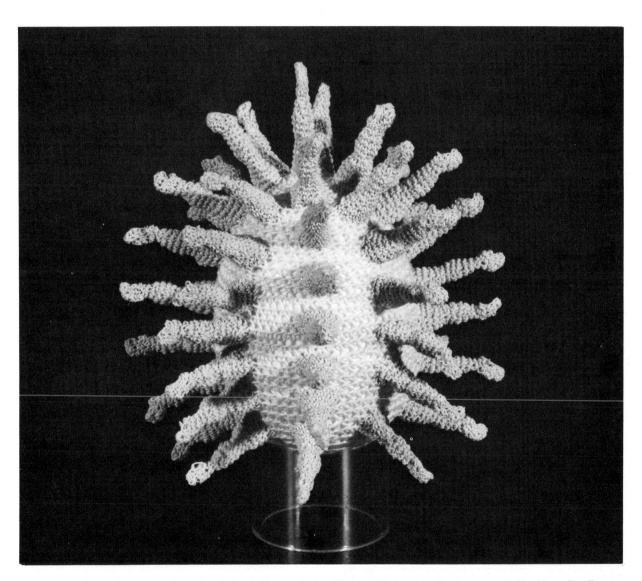

Legs II. *Crochet form mounted on plastic base. 6' x 7'. Artist, Norma Minkowitz. Photograph, Kobler/Dyer Studio.*

11 Jewelry and Body Adornment

If you like to create expressions with knots but do not wish to spend a long time making these items, jewelry and body adornment may be the answer. The finished piece may range from a macrame necklace, a decorative assemblage of different materials, techniques, and forms, to a fancy headdress or textural garment.

The techniques of knotting, looping, wrapping, and coiling offer many simplified ways of expressing one-self in jewelry and body adornment. Design variations—ranging from the subtle to the dramatic—are possible by combining different techniques or by accenting just one or several techniques with interesting materials and objects. Accenting with clay, bells, cork, beads, seashells, metal, bone, or feathers may be used to create, change, or alter the desired effects.

Vest. Detail. Knotting, ceramic bells, and beads. Artist, Carol Chesek.

Pendant. Crocheted wire form. Artist, Sarita R. Rainey.

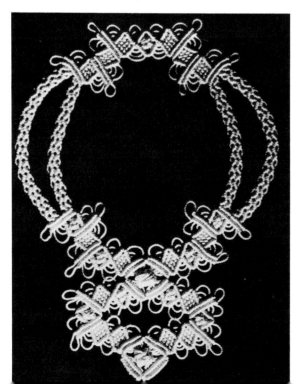

As a beginning, one might collect different materials, fibers, or manufactured objects and organize them into a piece of jewelry using any of the techniques previously suggested. Or one might choose to preplan an idea before starting to work. If the latter method is employed, it will be necessary to work in some sort of sequence, such as:

- Sketch a general idea of how jewelry should appear.
- Consider the size of the proposed jewelry piece.
- Determine materials to be used for repetition in contrast to variation, items planned as spacers between objects, and techniques for connecting pieces together.
- Select a process and technique that will best portray an idea.
- Organize a design focus of repetition in color, shape, pattern, or rhythm through size, shape, texture, and line; present a positive-negative relationship between objects and the surrounding space; work in color contrasts or subtle shades and tones.

Knot patterns often appear complex because they are made in layers. For example, sennits of knots may be overlayed by another knot pattern. When the sennits are separated from the front section and placed upward at the back, the major knot design becomes apparent. Layered patterns of this type also can provide a front or back ornamentation. They can be used to create an interest on the back, or they can be used as dangling forms around the neck.

Scraps of materials are cut into shapes, stitched on one end, and stuffed. Several layers might be stitched together to form a flat shape, or strips might be coiled and stitched in various ways to make a pendant. Knots, fringe, or loops add accent when stitched to the surface.

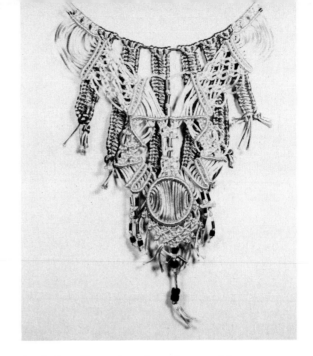

Neckpiece. Front view of two-layer necklace, knotted sinnets lie behind a lacy front of looping wrapping, and knotting. Artist, Betti Best.

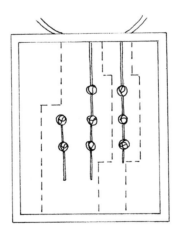

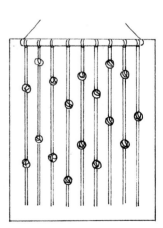

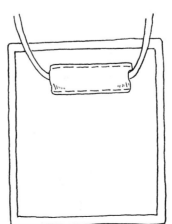

(Right top) Neckpiece. Felt layers stitched and stuffed with knotted accents.
(Right bottom) A strip of fabric stitched along edges may be added to back of designed shape for threading cord, chain, or wire neckpiece.
(Extreme right) Knotting on a background of felt.

89

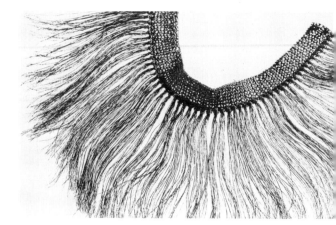

Choker. Crochet using gold lamé yarn and knotted fringe. Artist, Ruth Nivola. Photograph, Gwenn Thomas.

Stuffed shape accented with stitchery and knotting. Student, grade 10, West Hartford, Connecticut. Teacher, Barbara Rouleau.

Bracelet. Crochet. Artist, Ruth Nivola. Photograph, Gwenn Thomas.

Other types of loop construction used as body adornment are crocheted neck and arm bands edged in fringe or flowing tassels, wire looped with crochet or knit lace, crochet or knit pendants, or stuffed and coiled collars.

To make your own inventive looped bands, follow the basic stitch suggestions given for crochet. Even simple chain stitches can be combined to create bands of lacy patterns. Interesting threads in silver and gold will afford an elegance to these fabrications of soft jewelry. Accenting with wrapping, knotting, and beads extends the design potential.

An interesting jewelry effect is possible with crocheted or knit wire. Different patterns develop from loose or tight loops or a combination of the two. Stringing metallics in metal, paper, board, sequins, bells, or crystal beads add other potential accents.

Neckpiece. Wrapped cords curved into shapes and connected with stitching. Frayed cords provide texture. Artist, Sarita R. Rainey.

90

Jewelry Mounts

The mount on which the knotting, wrapping, or coiling is attached becomes essential to the total design. Each must work together as a unit.

In the example showing the triple framework of wire, the knotting conforms to the mount both in the way the cords are attached and also in the way the curves are repeated. Similarly, the example shown of a partially exposed mount relates its curves to the frame and the circle pattern where cords are attached.

When the frame is made first, the design and the supporting framework should relate to each other. In this case, the mount would conform to the preplanned idea. The example shown of a wire circle illustrates how a simple beginning can be expanded to create a design. One wire circle with two circles soldered to it presents a good base for the neckpiece as well as the pendant; one circle serves as a pendant base and incorporates a repeat of this circle on each side of the neck design. The neck part is added last.

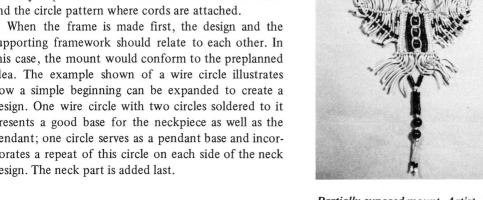

Partially exposed mount. Artist, Betti Best.

Designing around three wire circles. Artist, Betti Best.

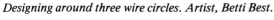

Triple wire bent into triple mount. Artist, Betti Best.

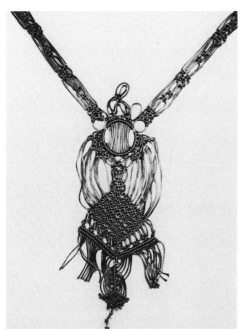

91

Likewise, color of mount and fiber are often repeated. For example, the blues of a metal enamel might be repeated in the knotting to accent the cord pattern. Beads could add further accents or add to the total design as they are threaded onto the cord. For threading, the cord may be stiffened by twisting and dipping into nail lacquer, hot paraffin, or clear or white glue. Thin wire may substitute for the holding cord or mount, offering more rigidity for the jewelry piece and easier mounting of beads, buttons, and the like.

Holding cords of various types may be selected by matching the cord to fit accents or knots. Some possibilities are twine, plastic fishing line, shoelaces, elastic thread, and various commercial cords. The use of more than one strand of cord adds strength and, in some cases, permits safety when a single strand might break.

Fasteners on jewelry take many forms: tied cords, hooks and eyes, loops and interlocked wires, buttons or fasteners of cord loops and twig, and wood or metal rod catches.

Neckwear may begin with the fastener, or the fastener may be worked out last. Sometimes fasteners are considered in planning the piece; or they may be determined when the design is complete. However, neckpieces often begin from the center armature, the knotting worked from the middle, and the neck part added when finished. Neckware may also be designed without fasteners, the necklace opening being large enough to slip over the head.

A holding element for a neckpiece can be a simple circular cord. To begin such a piece, draw a pattern of the shape desired and use the pattern as a guide, placing the cord on top of it. Tie the cord lightly so it will keep its circular shape. Beads or other accents may be strung on the cord to develop the design. Areas between the accents can be filled with knots or left as cord strands.

As you make knot jewelry, more ways of using knot ideas will become apparent. Sennits may be crossed and worked into bands of square knots; overhand knots may be used for fringe; knots may be worked over wire, enameled metal, or wooden shapes; and knots may be combined with crocheting, weaving, or knitting.

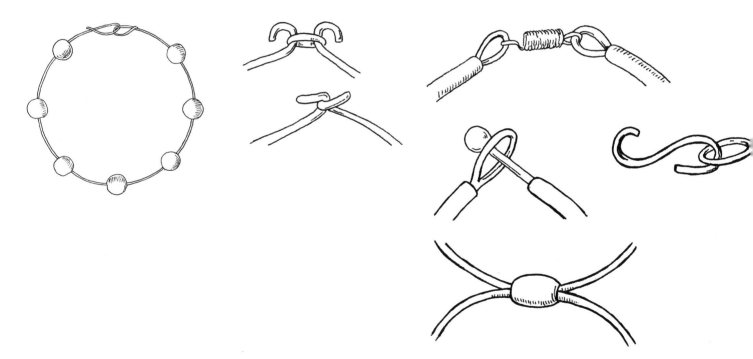

Bracelet. Looped and knotted leather strands. Artist, Temple Bruner.

Beads

Beads are one of the best items to provide accent and may be employed to create repetition of pattern, color, and texture. Commercially made beads are available from many sources, such as department, hardware, and variety stores; hobby shops; and school supply companies. Beads also may be purchased in necklace strands and later cut apart for individual use.

Some beads, because of their small, tiny holes, require extra thin cords or threads for stringing. Others, like bamboo, donkey, and some wooden beads, should be strung on strong, heavy cords, depending upon the weight of the bead and the number of beads combined.

Handmade beads come in different shapes and sizes. Color is sometimes added so the beads will contrast with the texture of the knot and color of cord. Making your own beads can spark imaginative use of jewelry accents. Small, in contrast to large, beads increase the textural aspects of jewelry; cylindrical ones interspersed with knobby, round beads provide a different texture. The material from which the beads are made offers still another type of textural contrast. Beads made of self-hardening or fired clay may be textured by pressing sticks, fingers, or objects into them to form impressions and roughness. Commercial modeling dough may be substituted for clay. With self-hardening dough, colors can be blended and white dough added to produce tints. When dry, color may be added by painting with tempera, acrylic, or dye.

Other useful materials for making beads are powdery compounds that mix with water and require no heat. For example, when mixed with water, instant papier-mâché will harden into a material that can be sanded, sawed, or gouged. Liquid compounds differ in that they can be used for dipping, dripping, or molding shapes.

Beads also can be made by wadding pieces of plaster-imbedded gauze and dipping in water, wadding newspaper and dipping in wheat paste, or combining sawdust with modeling paste to form bead shapes.

Simplified bead types can even be rolled from paper. To add color and simulate texture, cut magazine pages into strips, roll the strips around a rod (nail, dowel rod, or pencil), and glue the ends of the strips to the wrapped part. Remove the rod from the center and use as desired.

Beads also may be used as spacers. Spacers are items placed between other items or areas of knots to take up space. Items used for this purpose may be beads of various types. Also useful as spacers are seeds, buttons, tubing, washers, snap swivels, feathers, and knots.

Necklace. Beads integrated to contrast with thread. Artist, Hesi Bodlaender.

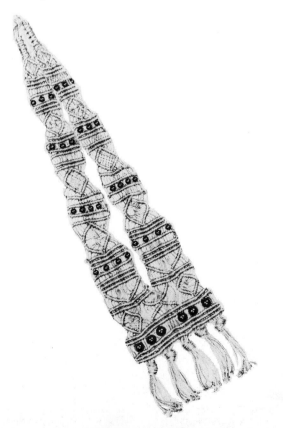

Jewelry Assemblage

Assemblage is not new to the designer, and especially not to the creator of jewelry. Sometimes defined as a collection of items assembled together, jewelry assemblage may be both two- and three-dimensional, depending upon the materials collected and the effect desired. These collections assembled as constructions may incorporate any of the design elements or principles of more traditional jewelry. Line, space, rhythm, and other elements may emerge as anything from spirals of coiled wire to elegant compositions in strands of silk brocade. With little or no change in design, a composition in everyday materials like aluminum wire and brass washers can be transposed into sterling silver and metal forms.

Artist, Kathy Muzyka.

Who would expect a piece of jewelry or other body adornment to be made of cardboard, cotton, silk threads, feathers, nuts, bolts, or washers? Assemblages of this type stretch the imagination—challenging the designer to explore the environment, collect materials, then select items with a focus on wearable assemblages. Experiment with different materials and techniques:

- Make cardboard foundations for jewelry shapes, then wrap or crochet over, around, or on the form.
- Wrap upholstery welting in different thicknesses, then coil and loop to create a wearable shape.
- Machine- or hand-stitch fabric and stuff to make coils. Accent the fabric with knots, tassels, and loops.
- Wrap or coil with leather.
- Cut pieces of burlap, felt, velvet, or other fabric and accent with coils, wrapping and stitchery, knotting, or looping.
- Combine knots and loops with found objects, with beads for accent, and to hold the found items together in a unit.

Artist, Claudia Budny.

Artist, Rachel Love Mitchel.

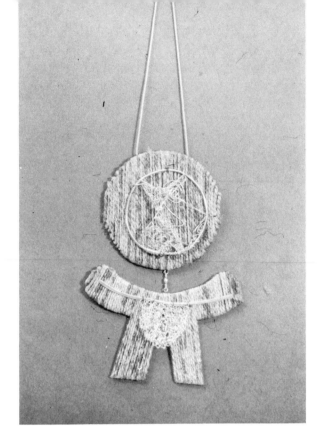

Artist, Marye Huldrum.

Artist, Jeanne Doyle.

Artist, Kathy Muzyka.

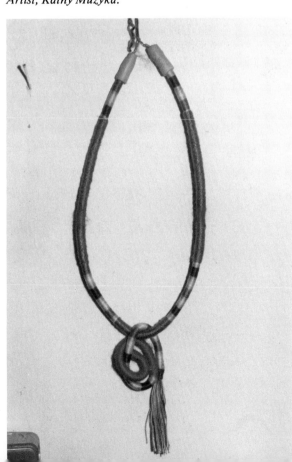

The procedure for making a jewelry assemblage is not difficult. In fact, it opens up many avenues for experimentation. What can one do with a piece of cardboard or with differing cardboard thicknesses? What can one find in a hardware store that will pertain to a jewelry idea? What does the fabric shop offer? Many items around the house will provide still other ideas.

Other innovative possibilities for expressions in knotting and looping are theatrical wearing apparel—masks, headdresses, tunics, and sandles. Stunning costume effects made by winding cord, interlocking threads, weaving, knotting, braiding, fringing, and fraying are only a beginning.

Although both costumes and masks may be constructed in innumerable ways, one might experiment making a mask by placing a plastic bag over a wig form. Select heavy string, binder twine, or thin rope, then dip this into glue and arrange as desired over the plastic-covered head shape. Hold in place with straight pins.

A female in my cap. *Mask. Crochet and knit. Artist, Norma Minkowitz. Photograph, Kobler/Dyer Studio.*

Headgear. Crochet. Artist, Norma Minkowitz.

When the cord is dry, remove it from the wig form, cutting away any remaining plastic that sticks to the shape.

The costume is often best made of heavy cords that will withstand wear. Lighter-weight cords may be used for accent or where strain will not occur. By drawing a simple shape as a plan for a garment and following it using half hitch knots and square and overhand knots combined in different ways, one may create capes, blouses, skirts, and cloaks in various styles.

Still other wearing apparel may be expressed in vests and coats, as well as in accessories. Different design effects are achieved through the inventiveness of the person.

Sandals. Linen with wooden beads. College student. Teacher, Nancy J. Koehler.

Costume close–up. Student. Teacher, Linda Eisenlohr Hill.

Cape. Student, grade 12, West Hartford, Connecticut.

Blouse. Crochet and knit. Artist, Norma Minkowitz.

Necklace. Artist, Carol Chesek.

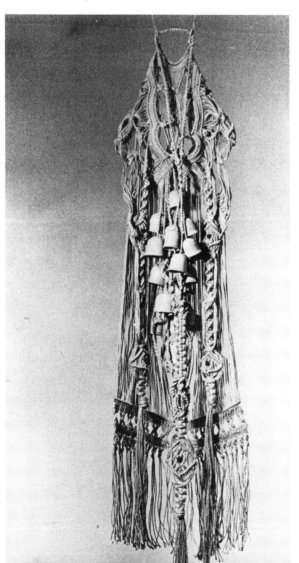

Vest. Front piece. Student, grade 6, Montclair, New Jersey. Teacher, Betti Best.

Necklace, braided, knotted, and wrapped in gold lamé yarn or fish tassel. Knots and tassels serve as accents. Artist, Ruth Nivola.

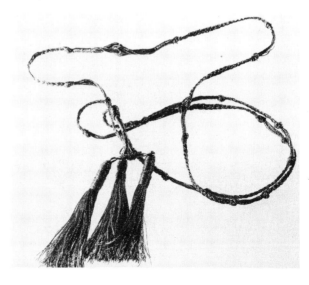

12 Fiber Sculpture

Sculpture, often considered in the context of metal, wood, stone, and plastic, is a popular new dimension in fiber. Fiber constructions using cord, yarn, string, sisal, and rope are often stretched over blocks, or balls; textured with different objects such as clay, plastic, and metal; knotted onto an armature; or hung as free forms. Working in sculpture involves one in the interplay of negative and positive space as specific constructions take form.

(Left) Construction. Cubes covered with cord in checkerboard pattern. Artist, David R. Cummins. (Right) Construction. Cord-covered balls. Artist, David R. Cummins.

Cropped Lingham. *Construction made of leather with cotton. 55'' high. Artist, Park Chambers.*

Cords in fiber sculpture can be attached to, or wrapped around, wood or metal rods, hoops of various kinds, and wheel shapes. Wire constructions become structures for holding or attaching threads. Also, wire, bending outward and inward to give form, can become an armature as it is run through a knotted construction.

Still another knotted construction can be made over an underlying support such as a bottle or gourd. For example, a knotting may begin by forming a circle of cord around the top and tying it in a knot. The circle becomes the holding cord onto which additional strands are attached. Similarly, a cord is formed into a circle with strands tied to it, then placed over the top of a gourd, which serves as an armature. A pebbly texture illustrates not only the circle of cord, with additional strands attached, but also the supporting gourd incorporated into the design. Finally, bottles exposed under and supporting a design can become an integral part of a knot pattern.

Fiber sculpture. Artist, Nancy J. Koehler.

Knotted hanging around two pieces of plastic tubing that enclose wire for strength. Beads attached around tube rings. Artist, Nancy R. Yost.

Cord wrapped around wire armature with fibers stretched across space between. Some wire is exposed. Artist, Betti Best.

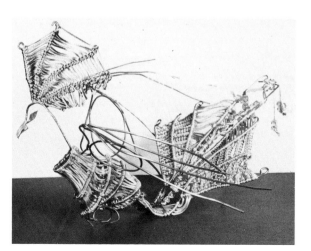

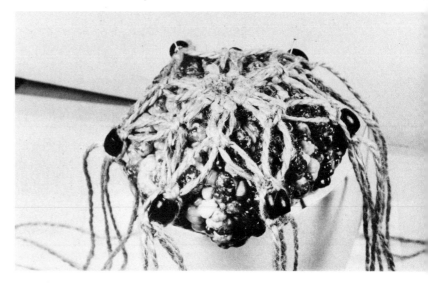

Student, grade 7, Montclair, New Jersey. Teacher, Betti Best.

Student, grade 7, Montclair, New Jersey. Teacher, Eileen Scally. Design started by knotting onto a circular holding cord at top of bottle.

The Warrior #2. *Artist, Lea Jones.*

(Left) Student, grade 5, Montclair, New Jersey. Teacher, Betti Best.
(Right) Student, grade 5, Montclair, New Jersey. Teacher, Betti Best.

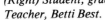

Fiber sculpture can have depth as well as length and width. It can cast shadows. It can be looked at from different viewpoints—top, side, and bottom. Each side or angle should be aesthetic, well executed, and finished. As the piece turns or as one walks around it, one can evaluate the textural qualities, both tactile and visual. One can further consider if other parts might be added to make the piece more effective.

Sculpture can be an additive process of building upon, or adding to, or a subtractive process in which parts or pieces are removed. Although it may appear so, fiber expressions need not be made of a continuous thread, yarn, or cord. Like clay sculpture, more fiber may be added to the piece as one works. Often, small pieces are combined in different ways by adding several individual shapes to make a single form; also, separate crocheted rings are stitched on top of one another. The shape is strengthened by the alternating direction of vertical and horizontal rows of crochet.

Crocheted forms may be stuffed as a series of small parts, then arranged in a group to make an overall form.

(Left) Front view. Student, West Ledge, Connecticut. Teacher, Marge Curtiss.

(Right) Back view. Student, West Ledge, Connecticut. Teacher, Marge Curtiss.

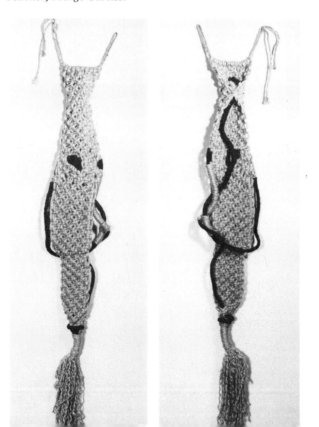

Whose Burden Am I. *Crochet and knit over plastic box and tubing. 6'' x 7''. Artist, Norma Minkowitz.*

Together with the linear fibers, the different directions taken by the small individual forms and their varying heights suggest movement.

A series of horizontal cords wrapped and connected to one another illustrates still another additive method. Sculptural forms emerge as coils increase or decrease in size, thereby creating a three-dimensional structure. The two small shapes attached to the main form become a single sculpture. The direction of the spiraling cords in a coiled form contrast with the vertical lines of the treelike crocheted sculpture.

Artist, Margaret Pelton.

Artist, Les Boknenkamp.

Artist, Gail Kindlund.

Student, grade 11, West Hartford, Connecticut. Teacher, Bernadine Bailey.

103

Artist, Gail Kindlund.

Separate parts are sometimes made by wrapping groups of cords or welting, then bending and attaching them as they are added to a form. The wrapped parts appear as thick lines, creating the appearance of linear texture, in contrast to the thinner linear texture made by the multi-yarn strands. Further contrast is achieved by wrapping the wood stand to give a horizontal line effect.

Interest in a sculpture can be created by stopping the eye momentarily at some point in the design. Notice how connecting one part to another increases interest as the eye scans the form. It also involves the viewer in open-closed projections at varying elevations.

A free-flowing sculpture may emerge as a collection of separate parts, all related in shape and color in low-, middle-, and high-relief surfaces. Some forms recede and others protrude.

Fiber sculpture can be many shapes and unusual in form, depending upon one's way of seeing. Experiment with different ideas and techniques. Try working in relief and in the round. Combine low and high relief. Build up a form by adding separate parts to a single construction. Make open and closed spaces that allow the eye to move in and out of the form. Connect parts such as head and body; experiment with color change to create interest.

Fiber sculpture may result in many imaginative ideas when one explores different methods of wrapping around a wire armature. For example, coiling, using various construction techniques, and employing different stitches are methods that might be used. Experiment to find ways that work best for you.

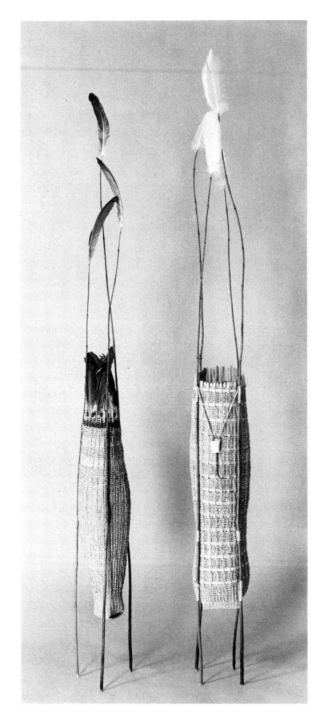

Dark and Light Spirit. *Twined raffia over flat reed spokes mounted on branches with chicken feathers and beads. Artist, Douglas Fuchs. Photograph, Douglas Long.*

Basket effigies. Artist, Barbara Wilk.

Crochet. Artist, Constance Lebovitz.

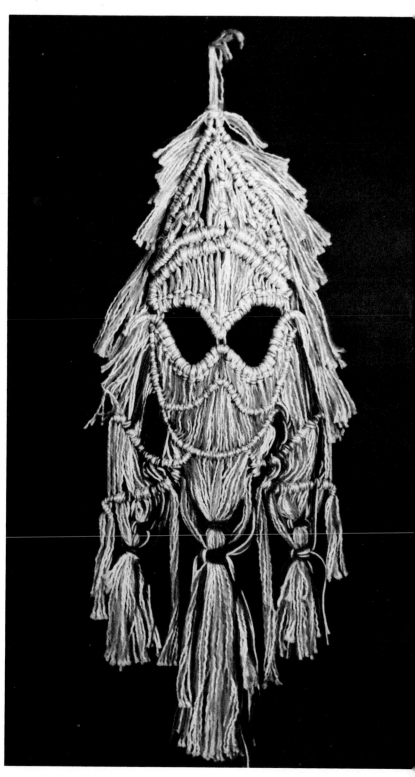

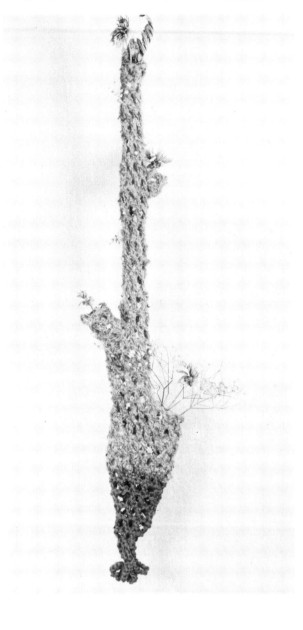

Woven sculptural weed holder. Student, grade 11, West Hartford, Connecticut. Teacher, Barbara Rouleau.

Knotting and tatting with no armatures. Artist, Joan Michaels–Paque.

106

13 Innovations

Other Expressions

Knotting, looping, and wrapping are used in innumerable ways to express ideas. The approach used throughout this chapter will help you visualize the essence of these ideas at a glance.

Experiment with knots or loops as accent.
   Paper made into three-dimensional forms with fiber, knot, and loop accents.
   Wood shapes with knot and loops as texture.
   Ceramic shapes attached with knots and loops.
   Ceramic forms with fiber accents.
   Dangling objects attached to knotted, looped, or wrapped fibers.
   Fabric relief sculpture and loop and knot accents.

Paper bag puppet.

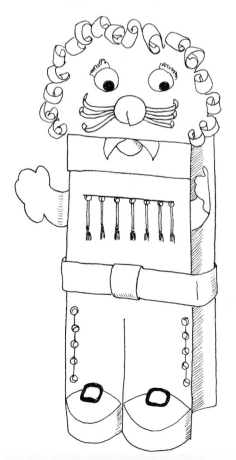

Knots made of strips of paper.

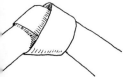

107

Shapes cut from rolled clay. Pieces are then attached to one another with knots and loops. Student, grade 11, West Hartford, Connecticut. Teacher, Barbara Rouleau.

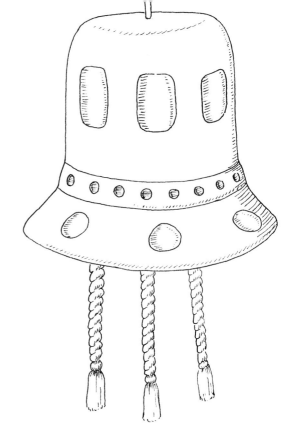

(Above) Ceramic lamp with decorative knot accent. Student, grade 12, West Hartford, Connecticut. Teacher, Barbara Rouleau.

(Below) Bell shape formed of clay with knotted clappers for decorative rather than functional use. Student, grade 11, West Hartford, Connecticut. Teacher, Barbara Rouleau.

Hand-built stoneware with hand-spun wool, horsehair, and shale. Artist, Lucy C. Driver.

Clay beads, knots, and strands of cord accent center of ceramic form. Artist, Carol Chesek.

Stoneware jar with polished knotted-linen top handle. Handle attachment on the side of the container creates further interest with clay beads, knots, and cords. Artist, Carol Chesek.

109

Knotted cords attached to thread spools. Student, grade 5, West Hartford, Connecticut. Teacher, Lucille A. Diorio.

Fabric relief sculpture accented with crocheted loops, knots, and metal. Artist, Sarita R. Rainey.

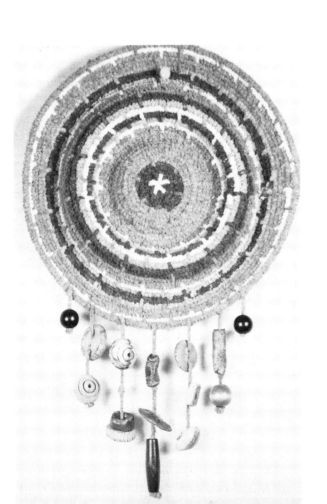

Coiled chenille form. Shells, clay, and wood beads held in place by knots dangle on chenille strands as accent. Artist, Harriett Winograd.

Accent knotting by airbrushing cotton strips,
  then employing them as a wrapping material.

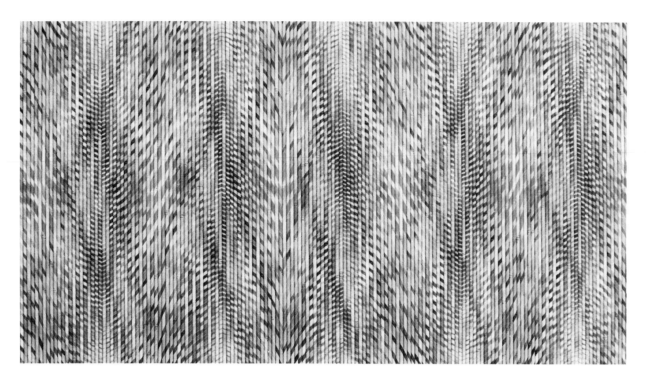

CISZA III. *1'' tubing wrapped with yarn and strips of airbrushed cotton cloth. 10' x 20'. Artist, Kris Dey. Photograph,*
Jan Stedman.

CISZA. *1'' tubing wrapped with strips of cotton cloth.*
5' x 5'. Artist, Kris Dey. Photograph, Jan Stedman.

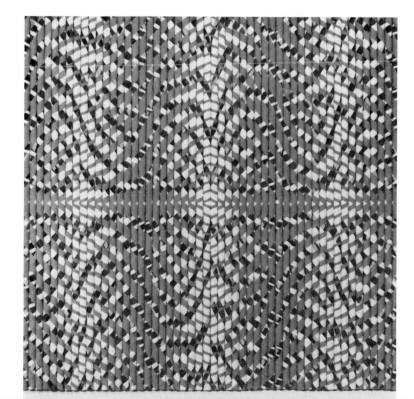

Explore the different ways to combine knotting, looping, and wrapping with other techniques.
  Combine weaving, knotting, and wrapping.
  Intermix weaving, crochet, and batik as a unit; or combine crocheting, knitting, quilting, and stitchery.
  Combine batik and looping.
  Experiment with crochet together with weaving.

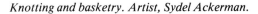

Knotting and basketry. Artist, Sydel Ackerman.

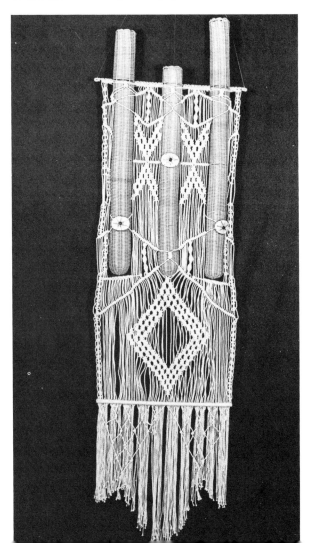

Student, grade 6, West Hartford, Connecticut. Teacher, Janet J. Farraris.

Horse Heaven. *13" x 16". Artist, Norma Minkowitz.*

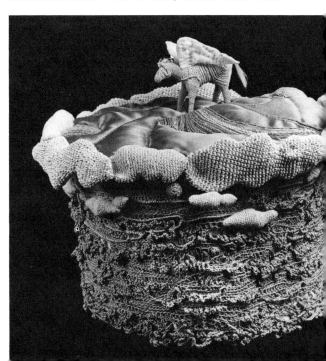

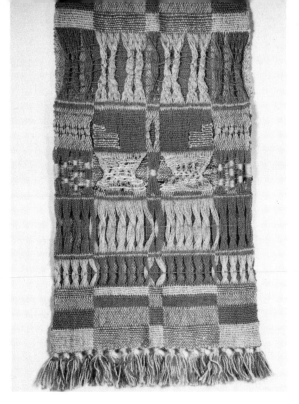

Weaving and wrapped threads. Artist, Betty Freedman.

Tapestery slit weaving and knotting. Artist, Chris Weiner.

Artist, Constance Lebovitz.

113

Peruvian gods. *Weaving, stuffed crocheted pieces, batik border. Center design accented with beads. 10' x 84''. Artist, Karen Chang.*

114

Tablecloth. Edges in tatting, stitched design using French knot. Artist, Ruth Rainey.

Batik accented with crochet. Artist, Holly Weller.

Artist, Sarita R. Rainey.

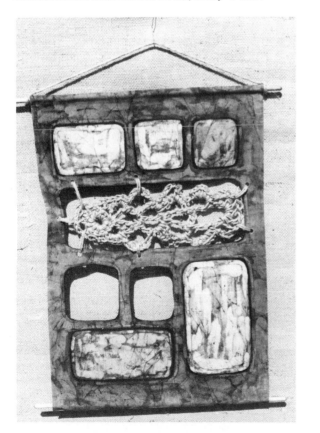

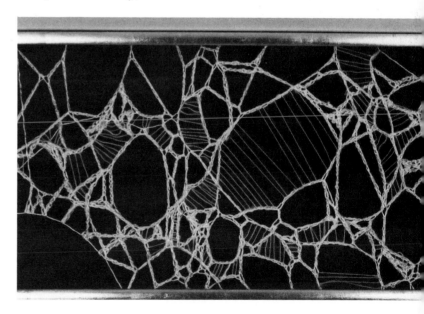

Use knotting, looping, and wrapping.
   To cover frameworks or objects.
   To finish a hanging.
   To create figures and forms.
   To make furniture.

Wrapping used to create rolling-pin cover. Artist, Harriett Winograd.

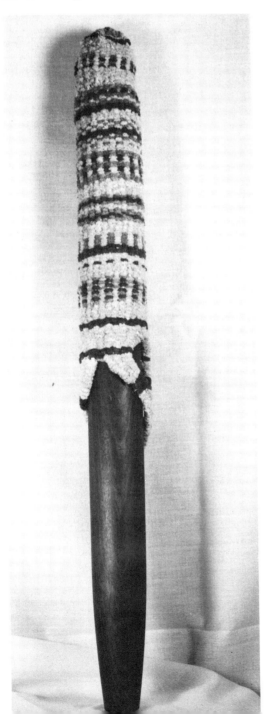

Lion. Knotted and frayed rope. Denmark.

Student, Lisa Stankowski, grade 12, Westledge School, Simsbury, Connecticut. Teacher, Marge Curtiss.

Student, grade 5, West Hartford, Connecticut. Teacher, Lucille Diorio.

Built from pine and poplar with natural linen cord. 28" high, 26" wide, 32" deep. Student. Teacher, Nancy J. Koehler.

Legereeder. Wall hanging. Double weaving on black-and-white warp. Seventy-two small tapestries combined into a unit. Knotted at rod with fringe. Artist, Ann-Mari Kornerup. Courtesy, Den Permanente, Denmark.

Hanging chair. Heavy-gauge white cotton cord on steel frame with orange rya pillow. 4½' x 2'. Student. Teacher, Nancy J. Koehler.

Trying scrolling with fibers or strips of fabric to form patterns as isolated designs or accent points as shown in the example of paper scrolling.

Scrolled pattern.

Experiment with different stitchery loops and knots such as the chain stitch and French knot.

Stitchery with running stitches and chain loops. Student, grade 4, West Hartford, Connecticut. Teacher, Lucille A. Diorio.

Knot or loop different materials.

Plastic-coated copper wire, knotted. Artist, Lucy C. Driver.

119

Sources of Supplies

While supplies are available at local stores and hobby shops, often one wishes to order by mail in order to acquire a specific kind of fiber or tool. The following suggestions are only a few of the many places that offer interesting materials. This list is by no means complete and should not be considered as an endorsement but rather used as a beginning reference.

AAA Cordage Co.
3238 N. Clark St.
Chicago, Ill. 60657

Cordage

Arachne Fiber Arts Inc.
217 W. San Francisco St.
Santa Fe, N.M. 87501

Fleece and roving

Belding Lily Company
P.O. Box 88
Shelby, N.C. 28150

Jute "biggie" macra-cord, Lily's rattail for macrame triple twist macrame cord, Lily navy cord for knitting, braided cord for knotting

Berga/Ullman
Box 831 L
Westerly Road
Ossining, N.Y. 10562

Swedish wool

Stanley Berroco
Elmdale Rd.
Uxbridge, Mass. 01569

Textured yarns for knitting, crochet, and macrame

Columbia-Minerva Corp.
295 Fifth Ave.
New York, N.Y. 10016

Rug hooks

Contessa Yarns
P.O. Box 37
Lebanon, Conn. 06249

Novelty yarns

Craft Yarns of Rhode Island, Inc. P.O. Box 151 Harrisville, R.I. 02830	Cord, jute, and rug hooking supplies
Dick Blick Box 1268 Galesburg, Ill. 61401	Craft supplies
Gloria's Glass Garden Box 1990 Beverly Hills, Calif. 90213	Beads and bells
House of Kleen P.O. Box 224 North Stonington, Conn. 06359	Imported wool, cowhair, and rug backing
J. L. Hammett Co. Hammett Place Braintree, Mass. 02184	Craft supplies
Ludlow Corporation, Textile Division Needham Heights, Mass. 02194	Jute
Norden Products P.O. Box 1 Glenview, Ill. 60025	Rug hooks
P. C. Herwig Co. 264 Clinton St. Brooklyn, N.Y. 11201	Macrame cord
Pepperell Braiding Co. East Pepperell, Mass. 01437	Braids and cord
Sheru 49 West 38 St. New York, N.Y. 10018	Beads, buttons, and trimmings
Straw Into Gold 5533 F College Ave. Oakland, Calif. 94618	Wool/hair and luxury and plant fibers
The Weaver's Shop Dept. FA 39 Courtland Rockford, Michigan 49341	Yarns for crochet and macrame
William and Co. Box 318 Madison Square Station New York, N.Y. 10010	Cords and twines
Yarn Depot 545 Sutter St. San Francisco, Calif. 94102	Yarns and beads

Bibliography

Anchor Manual of Needlework. London: Batsford Ltd., 1966.

Ashley Clifford W. *The Ashley Book of Knots.* Garden City, New York: Doubleday and Co., 1944.

Brass, Helene. *The Macrame Book.* New York: Charles Scribner's Sons, 1972.

Feldman, Del Pitt. *The Crocheter's Art.* New York: Doubleday and Co., 1974.

Graumont, Raoul, and John Hensel. *Encylopedia of Knots and Fancy Rope Work.* Cambridge, Maryland: Cornell Maritime Press, 1943.

Harvey, Virginia I. *Color and Design in Macrame.* New York and London: Van Nostrand Reinhold Co., 1968.

——. *The Techniques of Basketry.* New York: Van Nostrand Reinhold Co., 1974.

Holdgate, Charles. *Net Making.* New York: Emerson Books, 1972.

Horn, George F. *Elements of Design: Texture.* Worcester, Mass.: Davis Publications, Inc., 1974.

——. *Principles of Design: Balance and Unity.* Worcester, Mass.: Davis Publications, Inc., 1975.

Kiewe, Heinz Edgar. *The Sacred History of Knitting.* Oxford, England: Art Work Industries, Ltd., 1967.

MacKenzie, Clinton D. *New Design in Crochet.* New York: Van Nostrand Reinhold Co., 1972.

Malcolm, Dorothea. *Design: Elements and Principles.* Worcester, Mass.: Davis Publications, Inc., 1972.

Meilach, Dona Z. *Macrame, Creative Design in Knotting.* New York: Crown Publishers, 1971.

——. *A Modern Approach to Basketry.* New York: Crown Publishers, 1974.

O'Harcourt, Raoul, et al., eds. *The Textiles of Ancient Peru and Their Techniques.* Translated by Sadie Brown. Reprint. Seattle: University of Washington Press, 1962.

Palliser, Mrs. Bury. *History of Lace.* Marston and Company, London: Sampson Low, 1910.

Rainey, Sarita R. *Wall Hangings: Designing with Fabric and Thread.* Worcester, Mass.: Davis Publications, Inc., 1971.

——. *Weaving without a Loom.* Worcester, Mass.: Davis Publications, Inc., 1966.

Acknowledgments

I wish to express my appreciation to Dr. Robert Cooke, Professor Emeritus of Art, and Dr. Dorothea Malcolm, Associate Professor of Art, William Paterson College, New Jersey. Thanks also is expressed to those who willingly accepted my suggestions, philosophy, and techniques in their teaching of art in the West Hartford Public Schools. For special services I extend my appreciation to The Metropolitan Museum of Art and The Contemporary Crafts Council, New York.

Index